Claire M. Renzetti, PhD
Charles Harvey Miley, PhD
Editors

Violence in Gay and Lesbian Domestic Partnerships

Pre-publication
REVIEWS,
COMMENTARIES,
EVALUATIONS . . .

More pre-publication
REVIEWS, COMMENTARIES, EVALUATIONS . . .

"**A** fter a quarter of a century of sustained research, activism, and policymaking on domestic violence, attention is finally being devoted to violence in gay and lesbian domestic partnerships. This book contributes to a growing literature on the causes, manifestations, consequences, and responses to violence in gay and lesbian domestic partnerships. Taken together, the eleven chapters in this book present a plethora of empirical facts about violence in same-sex partnerships; identify a range of factors that render violence within the confines of gay and lesbian partnerships predictably similiar to domestic violence among heterosexual partners, as well as unimaginably dissimilar from that which occurs among heterosexual partners; critically examine the vast array of institutional and service sector responses that have been and continue to be used to control domestic violence among gays and lesbians; offer an analysis of the history of the same-sex domestic violence movement; and highlight the value of adopting an interdisciplinary approach to examining the social, cultural, and psychological context within which violence in gay and lesbian partnerships occurs and takes shape. Most notably, select chapters in this book remain sensitive to the ways in which gender and race/ethnicity interface with theory, practice, policy, law, organizing, education, and prevention and intervention related to lesbian and gay domestic violence. In the end, this book addresses an impressive range of topics and constitutes a "must-read" for academicians, clinicians, and policymakers interested in violence in general and violence in intimate relationships in particular.

Valerie Jenness, PhD
Assistant Professor of Sociology
Department of Sociology
Washington State University
Pullman, WA 99164-4020

Harrington Park Press

Violence in Gay and Lesbian Domestic Partnerships

Violence in Gay and Lesbian Domestic Partnerships

Claire M. Renzetti, PhD
Charles Harvey Miley, PhD
Editors

Violence in Gay and Lesbian Domestic Partnerships, edited by Claire M. Renzetti and Charles Harvey Miley, was simultaneously issued by The Haworth Press, Inc., under the same title, as a special issue of *Journal of Gay & Lesbian Social Services*, Volume 4, Number 1 1996, James J. Kelly, Editor.

Harrington Park Press
An Imprint of
The Haworth Press, Inc.
New York · London

1-56023-074-6

Published by

Harrington Park Press, 10 Alice Street, Binghamton, NY 13904-1580, USA

Harrington Park Press is an imprint of The Haworth Press, Inc., 10 Alice Street, Binghamton, NY 13904-1580, USA

Violence in Gay and Lesbian Domestic Partnerships has also been published as *Journal of Gay & Lesbian Social Services*, Volume 4, Number 1 1996.

The development, preparation, and publication of this work has been undertaken with great care. However, the publisher, employees, editors, and agents of The Haworth Press and all imprints of The Haworth Press, Inc., including the Haworth Medical Press and Pharmaceutical Products Press, are not responsible for any errors contained herein or for consequences that may ensue from use of materials or information contained in this work. Opinions expressed by the author(s) are not necessarily those of The Haworth Press, Inc.

Library of Congress Cataloging-in-Publication Data

Violence in gay and lesbian domestic partnerships / Claire M. Renzetti, Charles Harvey Miley, editors.
      p. cm.
      "Has also been published as Journal of gay & lesbian social services, volume 4, number 1, 1996"–T.p. verso.
      Includes bibliographical references and index.
      ISBN 1-56024-753-3 (alk. paper). -- ISBN 1-56023-074-6 (alk. paper)
      1. Abused gay men–United States. 2. Abused lesbians–United States. 3. Family violence–United States. 4. Gay male couples–Psychology. 5. Lesbian couples–United States–Psychology. I. Renzetti, Claire M. II. Miley, Charles Harvey.
HQ76.2.U5V58 1996
362.82'92–dc20
                                      95-52579
                                          CIP

INDEXING & ABSTRACTING

Contributions to this publication are selectively indexed or abstracted in print, electronic, online, or CD-ROM version(s) of the reference tools and information services listed below. This list is current as of the copyright date of this publication. See the end of this section for additional notes.

- *AIDS Newsletter c/o CAB International/CAB ACCESS . . . available in print, diskettes updated weekly, and on INTERNET. Providing full bibliographic listings, author affiliation, augmented keyword searching,* CAB International, P.O. Box 100, Wallingford Oxon OX10 8DE, United Kingdom

- *Cambridge Scientific Abstracts, Risk Abstracts,* Cambridge Information Group, 7200 Wisconsin Avenue #601, Bethesda, MD 20814

- *caredata CD: the social and community care database,* National Institute for Social Work, 5 Tavistock Place, London WC1H 9SS, England

- *CNPIEC Reference Guide: Chinese National Directory of Foreign Periodicals,* P.O. Box 88, Beijing, People's Republic of China

- *Digest of Neurology and Psychiatry,* The Institute of Living, 400 Washington Street, Hartford, CT 06106

- *ERIC Clearinghouse on Urban Education (ERIC/CUE),* Teachers College, Columbia University, Box 40, New York, NY 10027

- *Family Life Educator "Abstracts Section,"* ETR Associates, P.O. Box 1830, Santa Cruz, CA 95061-1830

- *HOMODOK,* ILGA Archive, O. Z. Achterburgwal 185, NL-1012, DK Amsterdam, The Netherlands

- *Index to Periodical Articles Related to Law,* University of Texas, 727 East 26th Street, Austin, TX 78705

- *INTERNET ACCESS (& additional networks) Bulletin Board for Libraries ("BUBL"), coverage of information resources on INTERNET, JANET, and other networks.*
  - JANET X.29: UK.AC.BATH.BUBL or 00006012101300
  - TELNET: BUBL.BATH.AC.UK or 138.38.32.45 login 'bubl'
  - Gopher: BUBL.BATH.AC.UK (138.32.32.45). Port 7070
  - World Wide Web: http://www.bubl.bath.ac.uk./BUBL/ home.html
  - NISSWAIS: telnetniss.ac.uk (for the NISS gateway)

  The Andersonian Library, Curran Building, 101 St. James Road, Glasgow G4 ONS, Scotland

- *Inventory of Marriage and Family Literature (online and CD/ROM),* Peters Technology Transfer, 306 East Baltimore Pike, 2nd Floor, Media, PA 19063

- *Mental Health Abstracts,* (online through DIALOG) IFI/Plenum Data Company, 3202 Kirkwood Highway, Wilmington, DE 19808

- *Referativnyi Zhurnal (Abstracts Journal of the Institute of Scientific Information of the Republic of Russia),* The Institute of Scientific Information, Baltijskaja ul., 14, Moscow A-219, Republic of Russia

- *Social Work Abstracts,* National Association of Social Workers, 750 First Street NW, 8th Floor, Washington, DC 20002

- *Sociological Abstracts (SA),* Sociological Abstracts, Inc., P.O. Box 22206, San Diego, CA 92192-0206

- *Studies on Women Abstracts,* Carfax Publishing Company, P.O. Box 25, Abingdon, Oxfordshire OX14 3UE, United Kingdom

- *Violence and Abuse Abstracts: A Review of Current Literature on Interpersonal Violence (VAA),* Sage Publications, Inc., 2455 Teller Road, Newbury Park, CA 91320

SPECIAL BIBLIOGRAPHIC NOTES

related to special journal issues (separates)
and indexing/abstracting

☐ indexing/abstracting services in this list will also cover material in any "separate" that is co-published simultaneously with Haworth's special thematic journal issue or DocuSerial. Indexing/abstracting usually covers material at the article/chapter level.

☐ monographic co-editions are intended for either non-subscribers or libraries which intend to purchase a second copy for their circulating collections.

☐ monographic co-editions are reported to all jobbers/wholesalers/approval plans. The source journal is listed as the "series" to assist the prevention of duplicate purchasing in the same manner utilized for books-in-series.

☐ to facilitate user/access services all indexing/abstracting services are encouraged to utilize the co-indexing entry note indicated at the bottom of the first page of each article/chapter/contribution.

☐ this is intended to assist a library user of any reference tool (whether print, electronic, online, or CD-ROM) to locate the monographic version if the library has purchased this version but not a subscription to the source journal.

☐ individual articles/chapters in any Haworth publication are also available through the Haworth Document Delivery Services (HDDS).

CONTENTS

ABOUT THE EDITORS

Claire M. Renzetti, PhD, is Professor and Chair of Sociology at St. Joseph's University, Philadelphia. She is Editor of the journal *Violence Against Women,* and Co-editor of the Sage *Violence Against Women* book series. She has authored or co-authored six books and numerous book chapters and journal articles, primarily in the areas of same-sex domestic violence, violence against women, the sociology of gender, and researching sensitive topics.

Charles Harvey Miley, PhD, was educated at George Peabody College, Baylor University, and Southwestern Baptist Theological Seminary. He is Professor Emeritus, Department of Psychology, Aurora University, Aurora, IL. Over the years he has maintained an active clinical practice involving cases of domestic violence, both heterosexual and homosexual. He has taught courses in gender studies and men's issues. He is a member of the National Organization for Men Against Sexism (NOMAS) and President of the American Men's Studies Association (AMSA).

Foreword

The field of domestic violence is burgeoning. Theory, practice, policy, law, organizing, education, as well as prevention and intervention efforts abound. Discourse is rampant, rendering those of us who strive to keep up with current debate, discovery, and practice running to catch up. Noticeably understated in the flurry of published work is that examining lesbian and gay domestic violence.

Thus, I jumped at the opportunity to write this foreword so that I could read what I knew would be a historical publication and thereby consider the wealth of ideas contained between these covers. What a gift it is! I highly commend it to the reader. The reading was a highly personal experience for me. I haven't written about lesbian battering for almost ten years. These papers inspired me to reflect on what I have learned in the interim that I might offer for consideration by the field. And I found myself arguing with a number of the authors, in my head that is, although my seat mates on the several flights during which I was reading the papers were acutely aware of the delight in the debate occurring in my mind. The pieces that critique the battered women's movement for our significant failure to embrace battered lesbians and fully engage with them in their struggle for safety, autonomy and liberation were profoundly troubling, and absolutely fair in their sharp challenge to the movement. The papers that reflect on the nexus between same-sex domestic violence and HIV infection are illuminating and invite practitioners

Barbara Hart, JD, is Associate Director, Battered Women's Justice Project, 524 McKnight Street, Reading, PA 19601.

[Haworth co-indexing entry note]: "Foreword." Hart, Barbara. Co-published simultaneously in *Journal of Gay & Lesbian Social Services* (The Haworth Press, Inc.) Vol. 4, No. 1, 1996, pp. xiii-xiv; and: *Violence in Gay and Lesbian Domestic Partnerships* (ed: Claire M. Renzetti, and Charles Harvey Miley) The Haworth Press, Inc., 1996, pp. xi-xii; and: *Violence in Gay and Lesbian Domestic Partnerships* (ed: Claire M. Renzetti, and Charles Harvey Miley) Harrington Park Press, an imprint of The Haworth Press, Inc., 1996, pp. xi-xii. Single or multiple copies of this article are available from The Haworth Document Delivery Service [1-800-342-9678, 9:00 a.m. - 5:00 p.m. (EST)].

xi

to investigate intervention and community organizing strategies designed specifically for the gay and lesbian communities. The articles that seek to build theory about lesbian and gay domestic violence give direction to further deliberations on the similarities and differences between lesbian/gay and heterosexual intimate abuse and on the cultural norms and structures which sustain or impede it. The papers collectively summon gay and lesbian people to work at creating intentional community in which intimate violence is eschewed, where mutuality and partnership are modeled, where the demand for an end to the violence is universal, and in which we diligently seek to protect and support the abused and call the abuser to account and transformation.

I look forward to the next dedicated publication on lesbian and gay domestic violence and trust that when papers are solicited for that volume, readers of this collection will have distilled the ideas birthed by these papers and tested some of the interventions inspired thereby. To facilitate this creation of new knowledge, refined practice and enriched community, I suggest that the reader convene a focus group among friends or colleagues and examine each paper both to expand the discourse and to enhance social justice initiatives.

Congratulations on this important addition to scholarship and practice!

Barbara Hart, JD

Preface

The publication of this volume is nothing less than a milestone for the same-sex domestic violence movement. It signifies the growing official recognition of domestic violence within lesbian and gay relationships as a social problem worthy of serious attention and intervention.

Space constraints do not permit me to discuss each paper individually in this preface. Suffice it to say that the papers address a wide range of topics, from a history of the same-sex domestic violence movement, to analyses of clinical issues in treating gay and lesbian perpetrators and victims, to the special needs of gays and lesbians of color and gays and lesbians with disabilities who are perpetrators or victims of domestic violence. It must also be noted here that although there is increasing recognition of the problem of same-sex domestic violence, most of the contributors to this collection were actively addressing the problem before it was officially "discovered." Some were motivated by their experiences as victims and survivors of same-sex domestic violence; others by their concern about domestic violence generally. All have been committed to raising awareness about the problem of same-sex domestic violence and providing services to lesbian and gay victims and perpetrators. The intensity of their commitment is reflected in these authors' papers.

Claire M. Renzetti, PhD

[Haworth co-indexing entry note]: "Preface." Renzetti, Claire M. Co-published simultaneously in *Journal of Gay & Lesbian Social Services* (The Haworth Press, Inc.) Vol. 4, No. 1, 1996, p. xv; and: *Violence in Gay and Lesbian Domestic Partnerships* (ed: Claire M. Renzetti, and Charles Harvey Miley) The Haworth Press, Inc., 1996, p. xiii; and: *Violence in Gay and Lesbian Domestic Partnerships* (ed: Claire M. Renzetti, and Charles Harvey Miley) Harrington Park Press, an imprint of The Haworth Press, Inc., 1996, p. xiii. Single or multiple copies of this article are available from The Haworth Document Delivery Service [1-800-342-9678, 9:00 - 5:00 p.m. (EST)].

INTRODUCTION

Shattering Illusions:
Same-Sex Domestic Violence

Pam Elliott

SUMMARY. Lesbian and gay domestic violence has shattered the illusion that gays and lesbians are less violent than their heterosexual counterparts. The reality is that domestic violence occurs at approximately the same rate in gay and lesbian relationships as it does in heterosexual unions. Many similarities exist, but the differences between same-sex battering and heterosexual battering are the reason this controversial topic has taken so long to address in both the gay and lesbian community and in the battered women's movement. New theories of violence and models for intervention must be developed if same-sex

Pam Elliott, JD, is President of *Alternatives: The Gay and Lesbian Anti-Violence Project,* Minneapolis, MN. She is also Founder and former Coordinator of the Domestic Violence Program, Gay and Lesbian Community Action Council, Minneapolis, and former Coordinator of the Lesbian Battering Intervention Project, Minnesota Coalition for Battered Women, St. Paul, MN.

Correspondence may be addressed to the author at P.O. Box 14294, St. Paul, MN 55114.

[Haworth co-indexing entry note]: "Shattering Illusions: Same-Sex Domestic Violence." Elliott, Pam. Co-published simultaneously in *Journal of Gay & Lesbian Social Services* (The Haworth Press, Inc.) Vol. 4, No. 1, 1996, pp. 1-8; and: *Violence in Gay and Lesbian Domestic Partnerships* (ed: Claire M. Renzetti, and Charles Harvey Miley) The Haworth Press, Inc., 1996, pp. 1-8; and: *Violence in Gay and Lesbian Domestic Partnerships* (ed: Claire M. Renzetti, and Charles Harvey Miley) Harrrington Park Press, an imprint of The Haworth Press, Inc., 1996, pp. 1-8. Single or multiple copies of this article are available from The Haworth Document Delivery Service [1-800-342-9678, 9:00 a.m. - 5:00 p.m. (EST)].

1

domestic violence is to be confronted. *[Article copies available from The Haworth Document Delivery Service: 1-800-342-9678.]*

DEFINITION/DESCRIPTION

The myth that lesbian relationships are more peaceful and egalitarian than heterosexual unions has been shattered by the reality of lesbian battering. Even the presumption that gay males, who are believed to be more enlightened and sensitive than their heterosexual counterparts, are less violent with their lovers than heterosexual men are with their lovers has been exposed as fantasy by evidence of same-sex domestic violence.

As the silence has been broken around the topic of gay and lesbian domestic abuse over the past ten years,[1] the disillusioning reality that gay men and lesbians beat, rape and verbally abuse their lovers has presented traditional domestic violence service providers and the gay/lesbian community with a troubling dilemma. What do we do with such embarrassing and perplexing information?

New theories of violence and models of service must be explored to encompass the uniqueness of same-sex domestic violence. Old fears of confronting arduous topics must be set aside if the gay/lesbian community is to incorporate healthy relationships, respond to victimization in gay and lesbian relationships, and render heterosexual domestic violence programs inclusive in their services.

IS GAY AND LESBIAN DOMESTIC VIOLENCE REALLY A PROBLEM?

Preliminary studies show that 22% to 46% of all lesbians have been in a physically violent same-sex relationship. Coleman (1990) found that of the 90 lesbian couples surveyed, 46% experienced repeated acts of violence in their relationships. Brand and Kidd (1986) found an incidence rate of 25% who reported that they had been physically abused by a lesbian partner in their past, while Lie, Schilit, Bush, Montagne, and Reyes (1991) found 26% reporting abuse (physical, sexual or emotional) in their current relationship. The Kelly and Warshafsky study (1987) of self-selected lesbians and gay men showed 46% used physical aggression for conflict resolution with their partners, and the Gay and Lesbian Community Action Council (1987) found that 22% of the 900 lesbians surveyed in the Twin Cities area of Minnesota had been in a physically violent lesbian relationship.

In the Gay and Lesbian Community Action Council survey, one of the few prevalence statistics on gay male violence showed that of the 1,000 gay men surveyed, 17% reported having been in a physically violent gay relationship.[2] This general survey, which covered a wide range of topics, included no explanation to survey respondents for its question, "Have you ever been in a physically violent lesbian or gay relationship?"

Though there has been little interest and limited funding to study same-sex domestic violence, especially gay male partner abuse, these few studies do indicate that gay and lesbian domestic violence does exist, probably at the same incidence rate as heterosexual domestic violence.[3] It is important to note that almost all of these studies relate to physical violence and do not claim to develop statistical information on emotional, verbal or psychological abuse, which would significantly increase the incidence rate. In the 1987 Lesbian Battering Intervention Project Survey in Minnesota[4] (Elliott, 1990), 76% of lesbian respondents had experienced some indirect threat of violence from a lesbian partner. In the Lie et al. (1991) study, 73% of the 169 lesbians surveyed reported experiencing some form of abuse in a lesbian relationship.

WHAT IS GAY AND LESBIAN DOMESTIC VIOLENCE?

The phenomenon of same-sex domestic violence illustrates that routine, intentional intimidation through abusive acts and words is not a gender issue, but a power issue. A certain number of people, given the opportunity to get away with abusing their partners, will do so because they hunger for control over some part of their lives, lives over which they feel they have no control. This perceived lack of power allows abusers to escape from responsibility for their actions. Sexism creates the opportunity for heterosexual men to abuse their partners, and homophobia, a tool of sexism, creates the opportunity for gays and lesbians to abuse their partners. Some heterosexual men abuse their partners because they can get away with it in our sexist society, and some lesbians and gay men abuse their partners because they can get away with it in our homophobic society.

Clinical work and advocacy with victims/survivors of same-sex domestic violence show that the types of abuse that lesbians and gay men endure are the same types of abuse that heterosexual women suffer. Like heterosexual domestic violence, gay and lesbian battering also includes emotional, sexual and psychological abuse as well as physical abuse. The abuse can be verbal as well as direct physical contact.

Sexual abuse, perhaps the most understudied topic in same-sex domestic violence, includes any non-consensual sexual act (rape) or demeaning language, such as minimizing a partner's feelings about sex, withholding sex, jealousy and anger about the partner's friendships, or making humiliating remarks about the partner's body.

Emotional or psychological abuse can often be more intimidating than a direct slap. The abuser's goal in this type of abuse is to put the partner down through the use of insults or shaming language. Threats to harm pets or children of the partner, threats to kill oneself, manipulative lies, and control of finances and friends are common means of emotional abuse. A unique type of psychological abuse for gays and lesbians is the threat of "outing" to family, landlords, employers, or others. This "blackmail" potential for same-sex abusers often isolates gay and lesbian victims to a greater extent than their heterosexual female counterparts.

The dynamics of same-sex domestic violence are likewise similar to that of heterosexual battering. Abuse often occurs in a cyclic fashion with a "honeymoon" period following a violent episode. A desire for power and control drive the abuser to beat, insult, or threaten the victim into submission to her or his wishes.

While much same-sex domestic violence has been found to follow the patterns of heterosexual battering, initial clinical and advocacy work with victims/survivors and batterers has revealed some crucial differences. The most obvious and most troublesome difference for traditional battered women's advocates is that the opportunity to abuse goes both ways with lesbians and gay men. Though mutual abuse or mutual combat are myths designed to prevent battered gays and lesbians from receiving services,[5] it is true that both partners have the opportunity to get away with battering in same-sex relationships. One may be abused in a first relationship and then batter in the next. Or one may be abused for months or years in a relationship and then, after the batterer receives help to stop her or his violent behaviors, the victim becomes abusive to the former batterer. At any one time, however, there must be a primary aggressor to exhibit power and control. Though infrequent in occurrence, the power base can shift in same-sex relationships.[6]

Myths also prevail which seek to minimize same-sex battering. If "boys will be boys" and "women can't really harm one another," then why put any energy into confronting same-sex domestic violence? In fact, lesbians and gay men abuse their partners in the same manner heterosexual men abuse their partners. Abusers of any sexual orientation rape, beat, insult, and sometimes kill their victims. However, seeking help as a gay or lesbian victim is tantamount to "coming out," and a major life decision. Most state statutes on domestic violence are not inclusive of gays and lesbians, and words such as "spouse" and "battered wife" remain on the books (Robson, 1992).

Another disparity for gays and lesbians, especially those of color or those from rural locations, is the extreme degree of isolation gay and lesbian victims feel. All battering victims perceive isolation, but gays and lesbians who have no hope of asking for help because of a lack of civil rights protection,[7] and because of having no access to the legal system by definition, are the most isolated victims in society. Gay and lesbian victims are beaten by their lovers and then re-victimized by the state. Many gay/lesbian victims tell advocates that they do not complain about the abuse because being victimized by their lover is less frightening than being victimized by the system.

There are a plethora of reasons gays and lesbians stay in violent relationships. Many stay for the same reasons heterosexual women stay: for example, love for the batterer, fear of reprisal, self-blame, and belief in their ability to change the batterer. For gays and lesbians, to those reasons must be added the inability to find help to leave and the unique potential for blackmail concerning the victim's sexual orientation. Many gays and lesbians stay with violent partners because to leave will cost them their family, their job, everything they have worked for their entire lives, should the batterer reveal their homosexuality where it is not known.

WHY HAS IT TAKEN SO LONG TO BEGIN
TO ADDRESS SAME-SEX DOMESTIC VIOLENCE?

For well over 25 years, heterosexual women have received advocacy, support and intervention from the battered women's movement when they have sought help. While the hundreds of battered women's programs around the country have championed the cause of healthy relationships for heterosexual women, they have been quite hesitant to address battering among lesbians. Most of the nation's programs still refuse to deal with gay male couple violence, even as a few programs begin to confront lesbian battering.

Of course, homophobia is just as rampant in these programs as it is in the general public, but many battered women's program service providers are themselves lesbians. These lesbians either spent many silent years hiding their own sexual orientation while on the job for fear of a homophobic reaction, or they chose to ignore lesbian battering when they were well aware that it existed. Those who did ignore lesbian battering, like their heterosexual co-workers, seem to have adopted the basic philosophy of the battered women's movement that patriarchy and sexism are responsible for all violence. Thus, of course, women cannot abuse and men cannot be victims.

Instead of focusing on the power and control issues involved in domestic violence, the battered women's movement over these last several decades has exerted a great deal of energy combating sexism, a worthy social problem to battle. However, by using domestic violence as a tool to fight sexism, lesbians and gays have been systematically excluded from intervention efforts. Because it was so difficult to explain away women as batterers and men as victims when using that movement's established philosophy of violence, gay and lesbian victims were purposefully silenced.

The gay and lesbian community shares responsibility for keeping same-sex domestic violence in the "closet." Though well-known as a significant problem for years, the community sought to keep this issue quiet due to shame and the reluctance to provide ammunition for the homophobic majority who would use such problems to demonstrate supposed inferiority. Gays and lesbians, even as they themselves were beaten, maintained the illusion that they were more enlightened than heterosexual society and, therefore, not subject to the same uncivilized behaviors.

The gay male community's time and energy were directed to the AIDS crisis through the 1980s, and to some extent that may explain why lesbian battering has received more intervention and attention than gay male battering. Also, in the mid-80s when the battered women's movement began to understand that lesbian domestic violence could not ethically be ignored any longer, the initial response was to open services to lesbian victims/survivors, still maintaining a refusal to acknowledge gay male victims/survivors.

Lesbians who were abusive confused traditional battered women's programs, especially when it became obvious that one could not tell an abuser from a victim merely by looking anymore. Even as lesbian victims have become somewhat welcome in many traditional heterosexual programs, the attempt was made to force these lesbians into the heterosexual models for service and accountability.

WHAT CAN BE DONE TO CONFRONT SAME-SEX DOMESTIC VIOLENCE?

When facing the reality of gay and lesbian domestic violence, we need to understand that simple solutions to new and complex questions will not suffice. Both the battered women's movement and the gay liberation movement must work together to rid themselves of myths and fears so that gay and lesbian victims are no longer silenced.

The battered women's movement must pay heed to new theories of violence which are inclusive, and they must stop their blatant discrimination of victims based on gender if they are to address domestic violence. The gay liberation movement must expand anti-violence projects from focusing on hate crimes, or the violence against us, to include domestic violence, or the violence among us, if a complete attempt is to be made to stop violence in our community.

Given time and cooperation on the part of the battered women's movement and the gay liberation movement, we will be able to develop new theories on the causes of domestic violence and new models of service and accountability that not only work for the gay and lesbian community, but benefit heterosexual society as well.

NOTES

1. The National Coalition Against Domestic Violence Lesbian Task Force initiated the first major step in addressing lesbian battering with the publication in 1986 of *Naming the violence: Speaking out about lesbian battering,* edited by Kerry Lobel.

2. Island and Letellier (1991) estimate that 500,000 gay men are victimized each year in the United States.

3. Violence will occur at least once in two-thirds of all heterosexual marriages and routinely in one-third.

4. This was a project of the Minnesota Coalition for Battered Women, St. Paul, MN, which produced the manual *Confronting Lesbian Battering* (Elliott, 1990).

5. This myth alleges that both partners in a gay or lesbian relationship jointly initiate the violence and participate fully as batterers.

6. Advocates who work with lesbian and gay domestic violence victims and abusers report that this shift is the exception and not the rule. Most victims do not become abusers, nor do most abusers seek help to stop their violence.

7. Only eight states had civil rights protections for gays and lesbians in 1993. They were Wisconsin, Massachusetts, Hawaii, California, Connecticut, Vermont, New Jersey, and Minnesota.

REFERENCES

Brand, P.A., & Kidd, A.H. (1986). Frequency of physical aggression in heterosexual and female homosexual dyads. *Psychological Reports, 59,* 1307-1313.

Coleman, V.E. (1990). Violence between lesbian couples: A between groups comparison. Unpublished doctoral dissertation: *University Microfilms International,* 9109022.

Elliott, P. (Ed.) (1990). *Confronting lesbian battering.* St. Paul, MN: Minnesota Coalition for Battered Women.

Gay and Lesbian Community Action Council, Minneapolis, MN (1987). *A survey of the Twin Cities gay and lesbian community: Northstar Project* (unpublished manuscript).

Island, D., & Letellier, P. (1991). *Men who beat the men who love them.* New York: Harrington Park Press.

Kelly, E.E., & Warshafsky, L. (1987). *Partner abuse in gay male and lesbian couples.* Paper presented at the Third National Conference for Family Violence Researchers. Durham, NH.

Lie, G., Schilit, R., Bush, J., Montagne, M., & Reyes, L. (1991). Lesbians in currently aggressive relationships: How frequently do they report aggressive past relationships? *Violence and Victims, 6,* 121-135.

Lobel, K. (Ed.) (1986). *Naming the violence: Speaking out about lesbian battering.* Seattle: Seal Press.

Robson, R. (1992). *Lesbian (out)law: Survival under the rule of law.* New York: Firebrand Books.

THEORETICAL PERSPECTIVES

Ruling the Exceptions:
Same-Sex Battering
and Domestic Violence Theory

Gregory S. Merrill

SUMMARY. This paper examines the challenges presented to current gender-based domestic violence theory by the existence of same-sex domestic violence. Charging that dominant theory is heterosexist and ignores the experience of battered lesbians and gay

Gregory S. Merrill, BA, graduated summa cum laude from Bowdoin College in May, 1990. Since February, 1991, he has been employed by Community United Against Violence (CUAV) in San Francisco, CA, as the Gay Men's Domestic Violence Project Coordinator. One of four of its kind nationally, the project provides counseling and legal advocacy to over 200 battered gay and bisexual men annually. For further information, CUAV's domestic violence project can be reached at (415) 777-5500.

Correspondence may be addressed to Mr. Merrill at 973 Market Street, Suite 500, San Francisco, CA 94103.

[Haworth co-indexing entry note]: "Ruling the Exceptions: Same-Sex Battering and Domestic Violence Theory." Merrill, Gregory S. Co-published simultaneously in *Journal of Gay & Lesbian Social Services* (The Haworth Press, Inc.) Vol. 4, No. 1, 1996, pp. 9-21; and: *Violence in Gay and Lesbian Domestic Partnerships* (ed: Claire M. Renzetti, and Charles Harvey Miley), The Haworth Press, Inc., 1996, pp. 9-21; and: *Violence in Gay and Lesbian Domestic Partnerships* (ed: Claire M. Renzetti, and Charles Harvey Miley) Harrington Park Press, an imprint of The Haworth Press, Inc., 1996, pp. 9-21. Single or multiple copies of this article are available from The Haworth Document Delivery Service [1-800-342-9678, 9:00 a.m. - 5:00 p.m. (EST)].

9

men, Island and Letellier (1991) have argued that domestic violence is not a gender issue and advocate a psychological framework that emphasizes batterer treatment. Examining the theoretical conflicts, this paper attempts to demonstrate that sociopolitical and psychological theories can be successfully integrated into a social-psychological model. Such a model, developed by Zemsky (1990) and Gilbert, Poorman, and Simmons (1990), is explored and critiqued as an excellent beginning. By integrating psychological principles and sociological concepts, this theory explores the many dimensions of power and explains the phenomenon of domestic violence as it occurs in all relationship configurations. Suggestions for further theoretical considerations and research are made. *[Article copies available from The Haworth Document Delivery Service: 1-800-342-9678.]*

One would hope that this article could begin without the assertion and lengthy accompanying arguments that same-sex domestic violence is a serious problem. Most of the authors who have written about this phenomenon make explicit reference to the degree of resistance to accepting the frequency and severity of its occurrence (Elliott, 1990; Island & Letellier, 1991; Lobel, 1986; Renzetti, 1992). In addition to the outright refusal of the lesbian, gay, and bisexual communities to organize around this issue, current domestic violence theory contributes to denial of the problem by failing to recognize and explain same-sex domestic violence. In this paper, I will explore current theory, particularly the tension between feminist sociopolitical theory and the psychological theory proposed by gay male theorists Island and Letellier (1991). I intend to demonstrate that the two theories are not mutually exclusive and can be meaningfully integrated into a social-psychological theory. This integrated theory, while in its early stage of development, has the potential to explain domestic violence as it occurs in all relationship configurations.

OVERVIEW OF CURRENT FEMINIST SOCIOPOLITICAL THEORY

To begin to understand the development of theory about domestic violence, we must examine the social and historical context in which it developed. Prior to the rise of the modern women's movement, the existing research and theories minimized domestic violence and, one way or another, blamed the victim (Martin, 1981). In the late 1960s and early 1970s, feminism flourishing in this country helped to change this minimization through its primary tenet, the personal is political. This tenet called upon women to examine the conditions of their lives, the roles assigned to them (and also made unavailable to them) in families, the workplace, and society in general, vis-à-vis men. Through consciousness-raising groups and efforts, women began to discover the many insidious ways by which they are made second-class citizens, subordinate to men. In particular, women who had experienced men's emotional, physical, and/or sexual abuse began to share their experiences with one another and, as a result, no longer saw battering as an individual problem. Women organized and politicized around the issue of domestic violence, defining it as a crime against women, and therefore, a women's issue.

Using the feminist lens, activists, researchers, and professionals devoted considerable energy to developing a feminist analysis of domestic violence. They determined that violence, the threat thereof, ascribed family roles, and limited economic opportunity acted together to further gender-based oppression. When looking for the root of domestic violence, feminists saw cultural misogyny and sexism. Del Martin (1981) convincingly argued that domestic violence is the logical, if brutal, extreme of sexist gender-role socialization. If a culture socializes its men to be brave, dominant, aggressive, and strong, and its women to be passive, placating, dependent, and obedient, and oppresses any attempts at androgyny or "transgendering," then that culture has effectively trained its men and women for bipolar abuser and victim roles, respectively (Gondolf, 1985). Men learn that it is permissible to use violence and that they are expected to be in charge of "their" women and children; women learn to accept that their role is one of a subordinate and a caretaker. According to this analysis, domestic violence is a gender-based phenomenon, a socially-based illness used as a tool of the patriarchy to keep women down.

Despite cultural sexism and the resistance of those who persist in believing that victims have some responsibility for the violence, this gender-based theory has become the most commonly accepted explanation for domestic violence among academicians, the domestic violence movement, and lay people. It has won widespread support because it coherently explains the phenomenon in a way which intuitively makes sense. While there is dissent (see, for example, McNeely & Robinson-Simpson, 1987), a substantial body of research supports feminist contentions. Coleman (1990) notes that most studies conducted about battering conclude that it is a significant problem that is almost always perpetrated by men against women.

While this theory is inarguably an important starting place, it leaves many questions unanswered and makes many experiences invisible. For example, as Island and Letellier (1991) point out, gender-based theory fails to explain why some heterosexual men batter their partners and others do not. Feminists of color also have argued legitimately that the theory does not reflect their experiences.[1]

With few exceptions (e.g., Gilbert, Poorman, & Simmons, 1990; Hart, 1986; Zemsky, 1990), most authors have not attempted to integrate the phenomenon of same-sex partner abuse into feminist domestic violence theory. Indeed, it is not easy to do so without contributing to one of the four most popular misconceptions about same-sex partner abuse: (1) an outbreak of gay male domestic violence is logical (because all or most men are prone to violence), but lesbian domestic violence does not occur (because women are not); (2) same-sex partner abuse is not as severe as when a woman is battered by a man; (3) because the partners are of the same gender, it is mutual abuse, with each perpetrating and receiving "equally"; and (4) the perpetrator must be the "man" or the "butch" and the victim must be the "woman" or the "femme" in emulation of heterosexual relationships. Although the body of research on same-sex domestic violence is limited, Coleman (1990), Kelly and Warshafsky (1987), and Renzetti (1992) effectively confront and refute the above misconceptions.

Robert Geffner, editor of the *Family Violence and Sexual Assault Bulletin,* expresses a common sentiment when he makes the following statement: "We need to learn more about this [same-sex domestic] violence and be willing to modify our theories and programs to include these 'exceptions to the rule' " (as cited by Island & Letellier, 1992, p. 1). Indeed, same-sex domestic violence, if viewed from the feminist lens, does seem like an exception. This is because sociopolitical theory alone does not fully or adequately explain why the same dynamic of abuse in heterosexual relationships occurs with as much frequency and severity in same-sex relationships.

PSYCHOLOGICAL THEORY

Highly critical of the dominant feminist theory, Island and Letellier (1991) break with it altogether. First, they assert that it is heterosexist because it fails to acknowledge or explain the existence of same-sex partner abuse. Second, they make the controversial assertion that domestic violence is "*not* a gender issue" (p. 255). Island (1992) believes that sociopolitical theory has led to ineffective batterer treatment programs and that treatment must be based primarily, if not solely, on the personality and behavioral characteristics of the batterer. Sociopolitical theory, he argues, has over-focused on the experience of battered women and does not focus at all on or explain the source of the problem, that is, the psychology of perpetrators (Island, 1992). As a result, Island and Letellier (1991) propose a gender-neutral theory of domestic violence which focuses on the psychology of the batterer. They provide batterer diagnostic criteria for the American Psychiatric Association to adopt and support its application to men and women of all sexual orientations. Essentially, Island and Letellier (1991) argue that the feminist lens should be replaced by a psychological lens and that batterers should be identified and classified by behavior, not gender.

While their objections are strong and have been controversial in the domestic violence movement, Island and Letellier (1991) have more in common with feminists than even they have acknowledged. They agree with the feminist analysis that victims are created by batterers, do not necessarily have pathology that led them to become victims, and are not necessarily in need of treatment (beyond counseling and advocacy to promote safety and to help manage the effects of the abuse). Interestingly, they also devote several pages to the discussion of masculinity as malignant, arguing that male batterers are unclear on the concept of masculinity, having equated it with violence. Finally, Island and Letellier (1991) note in the opening of their book that in heterosexual relationships where abuse is occurring, 95% of the perpetrators are male, citing statistics produced by New York's Office for Prevention of Domestic Violence. And yet, if their assertion that domestic violence is not a gender issue were true, one would assume that heterosexual domestic violence would be equally perpetrated by men and women. So, just as feminist theory alone does not fully explain same-sex domestic violence, the strictly psychological theory proposed by Island and Letellier fails to explain the disproportionate number of male perpetrators in heterosexual domestic violence.

INTEGRATING A SOCIAL-PSYCHOLOGICAL MODEL

What I would like to suggest here is that domestic violence must be understood as both a social *and* a psychological phenomenon and must be examined under both lenses simultaneously in order to be completely understood. Feminist theory and psychological theory are not necessarily mutually exclusive and do not have to negate one another. In fact, if synthesized, they can enhance our vision. Viewing domestic violence through an integrated framework permits us to see that domestic violence is a gender issue; that heterosexual domestic violence is, in fact, primarily perpetrated by men against women. We can also see that gender is only one of several determining social and psychological factors and that the absence of gender inequity, as in same-sex relationships, by no means precludes the possibility that battering will occur.

Zemsky (1990), in conjunction with Gilbert, Poorman, and Simmons (1990), proposes a social-psychological theory of lesbian battering which can be applied to heterosexual and gay male relationships as well. They separate the causation of battering into three categories: learning to abuse; having the opportunity to abuse; and choosing to abuse. The individual who abuses has first learned to abuse through a combination of three psychological processes, usually occurring in the family of origin: one, direct instruction; two, modeling or learning through observation; and three, operant conditioning, or learning by reinforcement that violence is effective and "rewarding." They also suggest that men might be especially prone to learning abuse because of sex-role socialization, but agree with Hart (1986) that women in our culture also learn and internalize relationship models that are based upon inequity.

According to Zemsky (1990) and Gilbert et al. (1990), learning to abuse does not necessarily lead individuals to enact abuse. For that to occur, they must also have the opportunity to abuse without suffering negative consequences. In other words, would-be abusive individuals must perceive that they can "get away with it." Because of the pervasiveness of cultural sexism, homophobia, racism, classism, anti-semitism, ageism, and ableism, some groups are empowered with privileges at the expense of others. For the battered heterosexual woman, the cultural context of sexism and other oppressions which may affect her (such as racism in the instance of a woman of color), as enforced by friends, family members, hospital workers, mental health providers, and the criminal justice system, contribute to an environment in which her abusive partner can batter her without intervention or consequence. Likewise, homophobia, heterosexism, and other oppressions operate in the same way to isolate the battered person in a same-sex relationship, permitting the violence to continue. While the social phenomenon of prejudice does not cause battering, it does create an opportune environment that supports abusive behavior by its refusal to challenge it.

Zemsky (1990) uses an apt example to describe the roles of actual and perceived power relations in creating opportunity. She writes that it is unlikely that individuals who had learned to harass the people with whom they work would harass their supervisors because the potential consequence of being immediately fired would decrease the level of opportunity. To extend Zemsky's analysis, if these same people were the supervisors, they would, in fact, be likely to harass their employees, because they would probably believe they could get away with it. To extend this even further, while these same people may not harass their supervisors, they may harass a colleague, someone at their same level of employment. They would be particularly likely to do so if they believed the victim would be unlikely or unable to report it and/or if they believed such a report would not be taken seriously or responded to. Thus, according to this model, abuse against someone with perceived greater power and/or the perceived power to bring effective, negative consequences is unlikely to be expressed, whereas abuse against someone with perceived equal or lesser power and/or a perceived diminished capacity to bring such consequences would be a more ripe opportunity.

Lastly, Zemsky (1990) and Gilbert et al. (1990) emphasize that although the learning may have occurred and the opportunity might be present, abusive individuals make a conscious choice to abuse. Although many abusive people may not perceive it this way, they have the ability to make alternative choices (or at least to learn alternative choices) and are solely responsible for their violence.

In formulating this theory, the authors successfully integrate sociopolitical concepts and psychological principles and begin to explore their very complex relationship. For instance, the learning process they propose is explicitly psychological since it involves the individual internalizing beliefs and learning behaviors, and yet, Zemsky (1990) and Gilbert et al. (1990) acknowledge that what is internalized is most definitely shaped by social mores. Their analysis of opportunity is largely informed by feminism and an analysis of power which expands beyond gender, including racism, sexism, heterosexism, and other oppressions. They argue that the social environment, particularly the relation of power and the ability to bring consequences, impacts how the potentially abusive person behaves. And yet they posit that this is not purely sociological either, because as important as the actual power relation is, the abusers' *perception* of the power relation and their *perception* of the partner's capacity to enact consequences (which can be distorted and different from the actual) are also important in explaining battering. Zemsky (1990) and Gilbert et al. (1990) close their model by promoting a psychological healing model, emphasizing abusers' complete responsibility for their behavior.

This social-psychological theory adequately explains why men predominantly perpetrate heterosexual domestic violence and why women are less likely to perpetrate. Heterosexual men who have learned to batter live in a culture which systematically devalues, discriminates against, and exploits women. In effect, misogyny and sexism increase the opportunity for heterosexual men to batter their female partners without receiving negative consequences. As a result, it is likely that these men would choose to batter. By contrast, heterosexual women who have learned to batter are not as likely to express abuse toward their male partners because their partners generally have more perceived and actual social power and the accompanying access to punish them. Instead, a heterosexual woman who batters might choose to express her abuse toward her children, siblings, elderly parents, or others whom she perceives to have lesser or equal social power and/or a diminished capacity to enact negative consequences against her.

Social-psychological theory also explains the existence of same-sex domestic violence by acknowledging the role of homophobia and by positing that the opportunity for abuse of power can exist not only when recipients have less social power, but also when they have roughly equal social power. This phenomenon of lateral abuse is especially likely to occur in circumstances in which the potential victim is perceived to be unwilling or unlikely to report, and/or in which the abuser believes reporting will have no effect. Like their heterosexual counterparts, same-sex abusers learn to abuse. Homophobia helps to create the opportunity for abuse without consequences by isolating the victims and preventing them access to resources such as their family, appropriate social services, and the criminal justice and legal systems. As a result, battered lesbians and gay men are unlikely to seek assistance, and even if they do, are not likely to be helped. In such a climate of opportunity, it is not surprising that lesbian and gay abusive persons are as likely to express abuse toward their partners as are their heterosexual male counterparts.

THE EXPLANATORY POWER
OF A SOCIAL-PSYCHOLOGICAL MODEL

One challenge to social-psychological theory is its ability to explain exceptions. How does this theory hold up if asked to explain the existence of domestic violence perpetrated against someone who has more power than the perpetrator? Specifically, how does this theory explain the occasional incidence of men who are battered by their female partners? Although most people know that a small minority of men are battered by women, this question and the challenge it poses to theory is rarely addressed. One answer might be that abusive heterosexual women only batter their partners in instances where they have or perceive themselves as having more social power, either economically, racially, or along other dimensions, and/or perceive their partners as being unwilling or unable to enact negative consequences against them.

While this explanation is plausible and remains within the framework of the theory, I believe we also need to add to our analysis a variable that is primarily psychological, the degree of severity of the batterer.[2] Those of us who work with victims and/or batterers know that some batterers will draw the line at pushing or milder forms of abuse while others will stop at nothing, the difference based largely upon their capacity for impulse control. I posit here that the more severe the degree of severity of the batterer, the more likely the batterers are to choose to abuse, regardless of the level of opportunity. For instance, a heterosexual woman who is a "severe" batterer with little impulse control might be likely to abuse her male partner, even though he has more perceived and actual power and can enact negative consequences against her. Because of the cycle of violence (Walker, 1979) in which the abuse escalates over time, the degree of severity might change across time and situations, making it difficult to measure. Other complex variables which influence degree of severity and make it difficult to measure include batterers' own shifting perceptions of being powerless and of not perceiving themselves as having resolution options other than violence.[3] Future work should develop the concept of degree of batterer severity and an appropriate measure, not only because of its explanatory value, but also for its importance to treatment considerations.[4]

I also believe domestic violence theory could benefit from further analysis of power. To date, the analysis of social power, as endowed or denied on the basis of gender, race, sexual orientation, and so on has been extensively explored and is useful. By contrast, the concept of psychological or personal power, referring to a person's ability to access the social and other resources available to him or her has not been adequately explored. Just as some of my clients are physically stronger than their abusive partners and could overpower them if they chose to, some of my clients are also professional gay men who have significantly more social power, and the access it affords them, than their abusers. However, because they have been manipulated emotionally by guilt, shame, fear, attacks upon their self-esteem, a distorted sense of responsibility and other complex psychological tactics frequently employed by batterers, many have been rendered powerless to use resources that are available to them. These cases demonstrate that individuals with greater physical or social power who do not have, or have been robbed of, their sense of personal power can be dominated by an abusive person with less actual power. In other words, the experiences of same-sex domestic violence victims teach us that domestic violence is not always necessarily about the abuser having more physical or social power, but is also about their willingness to use whatever tools and tactics they may have to subordinate their partner. Further attention to this less evident type of psychological or personal power, which is certainly related to self-esteem, will add a new, psychological dimension, strengthening the theory's ability to account for what otherwise might be considered "exceptions to the rule."

CONCLUSION

To conclude, this paper argues that in order for domestic violence theory to be comprehensive, it must account for both sociopolitical and psychological dynamics, and their complex, often intertwined relationship. A social-psychological model proposed by Zemsky (1990) and Gilbert et al. (1990) was discussed as an excellent starting place, and suggestions for future analysis, especially for measuring the degree of severity of the batterer and developing the concept of personal power, were made. As all theories must be tested, researchers are challenged to design tools for assessment and studies which will support or refute a social-psychological model and contribute to our understanding.

For those who strategize to stop domestic violence, the challenge is to devote ourselves to changing the social context so as to reduce the opportunities for abuse, including confronting oppressions, developing culturally-appropriate prevention and early intervention programs, and improving the legal system for all battered individuals, as well as developing a body of knowledge about the psychology of batterers that will aid individual, psychological intervention. If domestic violence is caused by both social and psychological factors, then viable solutions must address both. Finally, researchers are challenged to develop theories based upon behavior rather than upon social identity, theories which explain phenomena for every group that experiences it, not only the majority group. While these theories should not be identity-based, they also should not be blind to the very real impact of identity-based social oppression. These, indeed, are challenges to us all.

NOTES

1. A colleague of mine, Cara Page, instructed me in a feminist of color critique of domestic violence theory for which I am sincerely grateful. As Ms. Page brought to my attention, the feminist theory I have summarized here is predominately white feminist theory and does not reflect the valuable contributions of feminists of color. And yet I chose to represent it this way, exclusionary as it may be, because this is the most dominant form of the theory and the one most commonly subscribed. There is much to be gained from advocates for battered women of color and for battered lesbians and gay men of all colors working together to expand the current theoretical lens. To familiarize yourself with relevant feminist of color writings, see *Home girls: A black feminist anthology,* edited by Barbara Smith; *This bridge called my back,* edited by Cherrie Moraga and Gloria Anzaldua; *Mejor sola que acompanada: Para la mujer golpeada: For the Latina in an abusive relationship* by Myrna Zambrano; *Chain chain change: For black women dealing with physical and emotional abuse* by Evelyn White and others.

2. The concept *degree of severity of the batterer* assumes that batterers can be placed along a continuum of mild to severe depending upon their capacity for impulse control and the severity of violence used. This concept helps us to distinguish between batterers who have a higher degree of control over their impulses and use "milder" forms of abusive behavior and batterers who have little or no impulse control and regularly use severe, life-threatening forms of violence. I use the words "mild" and "milder" only to provide contrast between degrees of severity, not to suggest that domestic violence in any form, mild or severe, is minor.

3. Thank you to Beth Zemsky for raising this point in her critique of this paper.

4. Further attention to this concept, while crucial, is beyond the scope of this paper and the author's current level of expertise.

REFERENCES

Anzaldua, G. & Moraga, C. (Eds.). (1983). *This bridge called my back: Writings by radical women of color.* New York: Kitchen Table/ Women of Color Press.
Browne, A. (1987). *When battered women kill.* New York: Free Press.
Coleman, V.E. (1990). *Violence between lesbian couples: A between groups comparison.* Unpublished doctoral dissertation. University Microfilms International.

Elliott, P. (Ed.). (1990). Introduction. In P. Elliott (Ed.), *Confronting lesbian battering: A manual for the battered women's movement*. St. Paul: Minnesota Coalition for Battered Women.

Gilbert, L., Poorman, P.B., & Simmons, S. (1990). Guidelines for mental health systems response to lesbian battering. In P. Elliott (Ed.), *Confronting lesbian battering: A manual for the battered women's movement* (pp. 105-117). St. Paul: Minnesota Coalition for Battered Women.

Gondolf, E. (1985). *Men who batter: An integrated approach to stopping wife abuse*. Holmes Beach, FL: Learning Publications.

Hart, B. (1986). Lesbian battering: An examination. In K. Lobel (Ed.), *Naming the violence* (pp. 173-189). Seattle: Seal Press.

Island, D. & Letellier, P. (1992). An answer to Bob Geffner: Gay and domestic violence. *Domestic Violence Newsletter, 2, 4*, 1-2.

Island, D. & Letellier, P. (1992, July). *Battering disorders: Individual causation theory alternatives to heterosexist sociopolitical theory*. Paper presented at the Annual Meeting of the American Psychological Association, Washington, DC.

Island, D. & Letellier, P. (1991). *Men who beat the men who love them*. New York: Harrington Park Press.

Kelly, C.E. & Warshafsky, L. (1987). *Partner abuse in gay male and lesbian couples*. Paper presented at the Third National Conference for Family Violence Researchers, Durham, NH.

Lobel, K. (Ed.). (1986). *Naming the violence*. Seattle: Seal Press.

Martin, D. (1981). *Battered wives*. San Francisco: Volcano Press.

McNeely, R. & Robinson-Simpson, G. (1987). The truth about domestic violence: a falsely framed issue. *Social Work, 32*, 485-490.

Renzetti, C. (1992). *Violent betrayal: Partner abuse in lesbian relationships*. Newbury Park, CA: Sage Publications.

Smith, B. (Ed.). (1983). *Home girls: A black feminist anthology*. New York: Kitchen Table/ Women of Color Press.

Walker, L. (1979). *The battered woman*. New York: Harper and Row.

White, E. (1985). *Chain chain change: For black women dealing with physical and emotional abuse*. Seattle, WA: Seal Press.

Zambrano, M. (1985). *Mejor sola que acompanada: Para la mujer golpeada/For the Latina in an abusive relationship*. Seattle: Seal Press.

Zemsky, B. (1990). Lesbian battering: Considerations for intervention. In P. Elliott (Ed.), *Confronting lesbian battering: A manual for the battered women's movement* (pp. 64-67). St. Paul: Minnesota Coalition for Battered Women.

Definition of Roles
in Abusive Lesbian Relationships

Becky Marrujo
Mary Kreger

SUMMARY. Most studies of domestic violence, both heterosexual and homosexual, focus on two roles for the parties involved–that of either perpetrator or victim. However, research indicates that women who are abused, either by a male or a female partner, also often use physical violence in their intimate relationships. The present paper seeks to understand these latter cases by analyzing clinical data derived from the private treatment of 62 lesbian clients who self-identified as either victims or perpetrators of partner abuse. The analysis reveals that in addition to the two traditional roles of perpetrator and victim in abusive relationships, there is a third role, that of participant. Participants are lesbians who establish a pattern of fighting back against their partners with the intent to hurt and/or injure them. The clinical implications of these findings are explored. *[Article copies available from The Haworth Document Delivery Service: 1-800-342-9678.]*

DISCUSSION OF THE CONCEPTS

During the past two decades of academic, professional, and grassroots interest in domestic violence, the focus has been on

Becky Marrujo, MSW, is Director of Social Services for the Ramaha Navajo School Board in Pine Hill, NM. Mary Kreger, LCSW, M Chr SP, is on sabbatical from private practice.

Correspondence may be addressed to the authors at P.O. Box 57, Pine Hill, NM 87357.

[Haworth co-indexing entry note]: "Definition of Roles in Abusive Lesbian Relationships." Marrujo, Becky, and Mary Kreger. Co-published simultaneously in *Journal of Gay & Lesbian Social Services* (The Haworth Press, Inc.) Vol. 4, No. 1, 1996, pp. 22-32; and: *Violence in Gay and Lesbian Domestic Partnerships* (ed: Claire M. Renzetti, and Charles Harvey Miley), The Haworth Press, Inc., 1996, pp. 23-33; and: *Violence in Gay and Lesbian Domestic Partnerships* (ed: Claire M. Renzetti, and Charles Harvey Miley) Harrington Park Press, an imprint of The Haworth Press, Inc., 1996, pp. 23-33. Single or multiple copies of this article are available from The Haworth Document Delivery Service [1-800-342-9678, 9:00 - 5:00 p.m. (EST)].

23

exploration and explanation of heterosexual domestic violence. Much has been written and debated from the perspectives of two roles, that of the perpetrator and victim. Topics explored have included the severity, type, and frequency of the violent acts; the psychological characteristics of the perpetrator and victim; the effects of the violence on the victim; violence in the family histories of both victim and perpetrator; the criminal justice system's response to the victim and perpetrator; and many others. Given the adequacy of research findings on the above topics, few persons would disagree that most heterosexual violence is directed toward the female by a male perpetrator and that females sustain the most severe injuries. Within this heterosexual model of victim and perpetrator, the roles become gender specific. Whenever either of these persons comes into contact with a helping system or the criminal justice system their roles are defined by gender.

However, when researchers, professionals, and others attempt to apply this model to female-to-female intimate violence (lesbian battering), problems of definition become apparent. One cannot rely on gender to define the roles, especially when both women report using violence to resolve conflict in the relationship. In these cases, one needs a more precise and definitive explanation of the roles and dynamics of the lesbian battering relationship. As one searches the literature for more adequate definitions of the phenomena, one encounters the concept of "mutual battering," originally applied to heterosexual women, who use physical aggression against male perpetrators. This concept has been strenuously debated since its introduction. Essentially, the concept (as applied to heterosexual couples) promotes the notion that both males and females use physical and emotional aggression to resolve conflict in relationships. The use of the violence does not have to occur at the same time, and the roles of victim and perpetrator are blurred, non-existent, or fluid.

To support the notion of mutual battering, incidence studies which show that women use violence against men have been cited (Steinmetz, 1977-78; Straus, 1980; Straus, Gelles, & Steinmetz, 1980). To refute the notion, others concentrated on omissions in incidence studies, such as identification of which partner sustained the most severe injuries, which partner initiated the physical aggression, and the motive for the physically aggressive act. These writers noted that women most frequently sustain the most severe injuries, do not initiate the violence, and only use physical aggression in self-defense. Thus, two terms have been used to define women who use violence in relationships: that of a "mutual combatant" and that of a "self-defending victim." The mutual combatant has been defined as the woman who fights back and may at times initiate the violence, whereas the self-defending woman may use physical aggression to prevent further injury.

In discussion of the terms as they apply to heterosexual victims, Saunders (1988) raised the question of whether "fighting back" and "self-defense" were mutually exclusive terms. He acknowledged that many survivors reported a retaliatory anger at the time of the self-defensive act of physical aggression. He proposed that the terms were not mutually exclusive and that many women did not distinguish between self-defense and fighting back. His conclusions appear to support the viewpoint that abused women who use physical violence are "self-defending victims" rather than "mutual combatants." Renzetti (1992) stressed that not all violent acts are the same; that there is a difference between initiating the act of violence and using self-defense or retaliation; and that both severity of injuries and determining who used the violence in self-defense are important. Yet, in her study, she reported that 78% of her sample (n = 100) of lesbians reported that they had either defended themselves or fought back against an abusive partner. Of these, 18% described behavior that could be termed fighting back or "trading blow for blow or insult for insult" (Renzetti, 1992, p. 110). Lie et al. (1991), in a study of lesbians who reported being both victims and perpetrators of violence, reported that 30.3% perceived their aggression as self-defensive and 39.4% viewed it as mutual aggression.

Conceptually, both terms need further refinement and definition. Researchers and others do not address such critical factors as the motive of the abused woman (both heterosexual and lesbian), whether the woman's use of physical aggression is a pattern of behavior rather than an isolated incident, and the sequence of events leading to the act of either mutual combat or self-defense. Definition and measurement of the woman's motive for the use of physical aggression could address issues related to retaliatory anger, the intent to "get even," to inflict injury, and to escalate the violent incident. If the woman uses the physical aggression to retaliate ("get even," inflict injury, or to escalate the violent incident), is she defined as a self-defending victim or as a mutual combatant? Further, if the woman has established a pattern of repeated use of physical aggression, can she be considered a self-defending victim or a mutual combatant? Finally, does the sequence of events, specifically the initiation of the violent incident, define her as a mutual combatant or a self-defending victim?

These factors have not been adequately addressed for heterosexual or lesbian women. Critical differences between the two populations also need further exploration, especially in light of observations such as "the only difference in interpersonal dynamics and perpetration of violence in battering in lesbian couples is that lesbian women report physically fighting back more often than women who are battered by men" (Walker, 1986, p. 76).

DISCUSSION OF THE CLINICAL POPULATION AND THE CLINICAL PROCESS

The authors will present clinical observations on a total of 62 lesbians who identified themselves as either victims or perpetrators of physical and emotional aggression toward their partners. The majority of the women sought intervention on a voluntary basis, and a minority (11%) were court-ordered into treatment. The court-ordered population was required to complete 36 weeks of state-certified treatment on the dynamics of domestic violence. Other women were referred from a variety of agencies, including battered women's shelters, private practitioners, and criminal justice agencies.

The women, including the court-ordered women, represent a cross section of the population in terms of employment, education, religious affiliation, and social class. Of the 62 women, 76% were white and 24% were women of color (7 were African-American, 6 were Hispanic-American, and 2 were Native-American). They ranged in age from 20 to 51 years. Of the total, 34 women were living with their partners when they completed treatment. These women were seen in individual, couples, and/or group sessions.

Because of the authors' previous experience with primarily heterosexual battered women, they sought to address the issues presented by the women in the present sample from the perspectives of the roles of victim and perpetrator. The authors solicited intake information from these two perspectives. The initial interview and intake topics were developed with questions specific to either the victim's or perpetrator's experience. The authors accepted their self-reports and developed a treatment plan based upon commonly accepted models of support and safety intervention for the victim and confrontation and containment of the perpetrator's anger. A few weeks into the treatment, a percentage of the women who had self-reported as victims began to describe a pattern of fighting back during the violent episodes. After repeated reports of patterns of fighting back in the relationships, the authors revised their intake and initial interview questionnaires. The revised material asked more open-ended questions about the abusive relationship, the episode leading to intervention (voluntary and involuntary), and the pattern of violence for the couple.

The revised questionnaire asked the women to tell whether there had ever been either physical or emotional abuse in the relationship. Further questions asked the women to respond to the range of either physical or emotional abuse experienced (from pushing/grabbing to the use of weapons and screaming/yelling). The women were asked both if they had ever inflicted an injury on their partner (either emotional or physical) and if they had ever sustained an injury from their partner. The women were also asked to describe the last violent incident (the one leading to intervention) and to identify who initiated the aggressive act. In addition, they were asked to give their understanding of causation of the violent incident. Other questions were related to whether the police were called and the women's opinions as to whether this domestic violence incident required police intervention. Finally, each woman was asked if she thought she was in an abusive relationship; if there had been other violent incidents in this relationship; if her style of "fighting" had changed over time and how her style of "fighting" had changed; if medical treatment was ever needed for either partner after an abusive incident; and a description of other abusive relationships (if this was not the first abusive relationship).

The information gathered from the first interview was then used as a foundation to begin exploration of the abusive relationship. Other information gathered included clinical observations within the individual and/or group setting.

DISCUSSION OF CLINICAL OBSERVATIONS AND INTERVIEWS

Based on responses to the initial questionnaires, and information from individual and/or group sessions with their lesbian clients in abusive relationships, the authors found that a substantial percentage (34%) reported a pattern of fighting back. The term "fighting back" as used by the authors means a repeated pattern of physical and/or emotional aggression in response to the partner's aggressive act. It is to be distinguished from self-defense because it became an established pattern of response and is not confined to an isolated violent incident. Further, the self-reported intent of the fighting back during the violent incident is to hurt, injure, or get even with the partner.

The authors also found that 27% of their lesbian clients had many of the psychological characteristics commonly used to describe male heterosexual perpetrators. Similarly, 39% of their clients exhibited psychological characteristics most often ascribed to heterosexual victims. To clarify the various roles, the authors defined three separate roles for the lesbians involved in abusive relationships. The roles of *primary aggressor* (similar to heterosexual perpetrators), *primary victim* (similar to heterosexual victims), and *participant* (one who self-reports an established pattern of fighting back) were the terms used to clarify the roles assumed by their clients.

The definition of the three roles (primary aggressor, participant, and primary victim) allowed the authors more flexibility in the treatment and exploration of the dynamics of the abusive relationship. Briefly described, the primary aggressor role would be most comparable to the heterosexual male perpetrator; the primary victim most often would be the victim in the abusive relationship; and the participant would be a role that often contains elements of both roles. The characteristics of these respective roles are summarized in Table 1.

TABLE 1. Psychological Characteristics of Lesbians in Various Roles in Abusive Lesbian Relationships.

PRIMARY AGGRESSOR	PARTICIPANT	PRIMARY VICTIM
pathological jealousy	slight degree of jealousy	no jealousy
controlling in most aspects of the relationship	selective control of issues in the relationship	illusion of control
manipulative	selective manipulation about selected issues (finances, car, etc.)	manipulates environment/situation to maintain safety
highly intrusive into partner's activities and relationships	selective intrusiveness about selected issues	not intrusive
problems with anger control outside the home	minor problems with anger control outside the home	rare problems with anger management
high level of anger/rage	expressed retaliatory rage toward partner	internalized, self-directed anger (depression)
male-identified (privilege/status)	fluid	care-taking of others
self-focused, self-directed	fluid	other focused, other directed
little or no respect for partner's personal boundaries	fluid	doesn't assert boundaries
sense of entitlement	fluid	low self-esteem
avoids responsibility for behavior	will accept responsibility for behavior	overly responsible for self and others
feels more than adequate in the relationship	fluid	feels inadequate in the relationship

The lesbians whom the authors identified as primary aggressors exhibited many of the same psychological characteristics of perpetrators. They were pathologically jealous, controlling in the relationship, highly intrusive into their partners' activities, avoided responsibility for the violent incident(s), had a sense of personal entitlement in most areas, and were focused on their own needs rather than their partners' needs. They also tended to experience problems with anger containment outside of the home environment (e.g., at work or with other friends and family). They felt more than adequate in the relationship, blamed their partners for various shortcomings, and were male-privilege identified.

On the other hand, primary victims were generally depressed and felt inadequate in the relationship. They generally were not jealous, controlling, or intrusive, but they were overly responsible for others, and focused on their partners' needs rather than their own. They generally fostered an illusion of having control in the relationship and often manipulated the environment or situation to maintain their personal safety. Occasionally, primary victims reported "fighting back." However, further exploration of the incidents revealed that their intent was to get away from the primary aggressor or to attain personal safety. Typically, they had no established pattern of fighting back and no intent to hurt their partners.

Participants, as defined by these authors, exhibited some jealousy, but were not necessarily pathologically jealous. They were controlling in some areas of the relationship, but not overly intrusive and controlling. Often they experienced minor problems with anger management outside the home. They generally accepted responsibility for "fighting back" during the violent incident. In both group and individual sessions, they expressed a high degree of retaliatory anger and often rage toward their partners. They used language that was descriptive of their anger level and their intent, such as "I wasn't going to let her get away with it [the violence] this time." They also reported fighting back as an established pattern in the abusive relationship. In other areas, discussed previously, their adaptations were more fluid. Oftentimes, they had more characteristics of the victim than the perpetrator. But while they were experiencing "retaliatory anger," their language and behavior were more like that of a primary aggressor.

Usually, the primary aggressor initiated the physical and/or emotional violence; the participant did not initiate the violence, but had an established pattern of "fighting back"; and the primary victim neither initiated the violence nor had a pattern of "fighting back." The primary victim rarely fought back and, on those occasions when she did, it was only to secure her personal safety.

Other differences between the three roles are detailed in Table 2. These differences were related to how each woman responded to and handled the conflictual situation leading to the violent incident. On the one hand, the primary aggressor was interested in escalating the conflict and its resultant violence and was fully engaged in the fight. In contrast, the participant, once the conflict had been initiated, fought back for the duration of the violent incident and was not interested in disengaging from the conflict. The primary victim was interested in disengaging from the conflict, de-escalating the violent incident, and securing her personal safety. Further, the primary aggressor and the participant often reported feeling "victimized" by the fight, whereas the primary victim reported being "confused." Both the primary aggressor and the participant expressed much clarity about the actual violent incident(s), whereas the primary victim expressed confusion. However, the clarity expressed by the former was related to the motive for the violence, rather than the details of it. The primary aggressor often expressed victimization; for example, "She [her partner] did x to me," whereas the participant expressed retaliatory anger, such as "I wasn't going to let her get away with it." In contrast, the primary victim expressed clarity about the actual sequence and details of the violent incident, but not the perpetrator's motive.

Finally, the authors found that the roles of primary victim and primary aggressor were more defined and rigid than the role of participant. Often lesbians who were classified as participants described themselves as primary victims in previous abusive relationships.

IMPLICATIONS OF CLINICAL OBSERVATIONS AND PROPOSED ROLES

The proposed roles of primary aggressor, primary victim, and participant have been offered as an invitation to researchers and

TABLE 2. Descriptive Characteristics of Violent Incidents by Roles in Abusive Lesbian Relationships.

PRIMARY AGGRESSOR	PARTICIPANT	PRIMARY VICTIM
generally initiates the fight (verbal/physical)	may not initiate fight but will participate	does not initiate the fight
fully engages in the conflict	will fight back for the duration of the fight (verbal/physical)	does not fight back except in unusual circumstances and then only to defend self
interested in escalating the conflict	not interested in dis-engaging from the conflict once it has begun	interested in dis-engaging from the conflict
may call the police or crisis line after the incident	may call the police or crisis line after the incident	generally will not call the police or crisis line after the incident. May call if there has been some significant change in the pattern-degree of violence
clarity about the violent incident (motive not details)	some clarity about the violent incident (motive not details)	confused about the violent incident (details not motive)
feels victimized	feels victimized	feels confused

others to develop a more adequate and precise definition of possible roles assumed by lesbians involved in abusive relationships. The role of participant has been offered by the authors to explain the behavior of lesbians who repeatedly fought back with the intent to hurt their partners. The authors rejected the use of "mutual combatant" to describe these women because of the inadequacy of the term. Also, the term mutual combatant denotes equality in terms of infliction of injuries and responsibility for initiating the act of physical and/or emotional abuse. The lesbian defined as a participant did not initiate the violent incident(s) and did not consistently inflict the same level of injuries on her partner that she sustained herself.

Given the present paucity of information on lesbians who fight back and the roles assumed by those involved in abusive relationships, the proposed roles could facilitate adequate intervention. Use of the proposed terms would enable clinicians and others to more accurately define treatment goals and methods. However, like other summaries of clinical observations, the roles proposed by these authors will need to be validated through further empirical research.

REFERENCES

Lie, G., Schilit, R., Bush, J., Montagne, M., & Reyes, L. (1991). Lesbians in currently aggressive relationships: How frequently do they report aggressive past relationships? *Violence and Victims, 6,* 121-135.

Renzetti, C.M. (1992). *Violent betrayal: Partner abuse in lesbian relationships.* Newbury Park, CA: Sage Publications.

Saunders, D.G. (1988). Wife abuse, husband abuse, or mutual combat? A feminist perspective on the empirical findings. In K. Yllo & M. Bograd (Eds.), *Feminist perspectives on wife abuse* (pp. 90-113). Newbury Park, CA: Sage Publications.

Steinmetz, S.K. (1977-1978). The battered husband syndrome. *Victimology: An International Journal, 2,* 499-509.

Straus, M.A. (1980). Victims and aggressors in marital violence. *American Behavioral Scientist, 23,* 681-704.

Straus, M.A., Gelles, R.J., & Steinmetz, S.K. (1980). *Behind closed doors: Violence in the American family.* New York: Doubleday/Anchor.

Walker, L. (1986). Battered women's shelters and work with battered lesbians. In K. Lobel (Ed.), *Naming the violence* (pp. 73-76). Seattle, WA: Seal Press.

A Survey of Factors Contributing to Gay and Lesbian Domestic Violence

Ned Farley

SUMMARY. Gay and lesbian domestic violence is still a relatively new topic of study; work has been done in this area only since the early 1980s. Thus, little formal research has been published regarding this issue. This article presents a qualitative study of gay male and lesbian perpetrators of domestic violence. By using demographic profiles from 288 clients who had been referred for perpetrator treatment, the author sought to understand whether self-abusive behaviors, involving drugs, alcohol, food and sex are predominant among perpetrators, as well as to explore the prevalence of intergenerational abuse patterns. Analysis revealed a high incidence of personal histories of abuse experiences among gay/lesbian adult perpetrators, as well as a high incidence of secondary abusive behaviors within this sample. *[Article copies available from The Haworth Document Delivery Service: 1-800-342-9678.]*

Ned Farley, PhD, is a core faculty member of the Masters in Psychology Program at Antioch University-Seattle, and a psychotherapist in private practice. He received his doctorate in Counseling Psychology at The Union Institute.

Correspondence may be addressed to the author at Antioch University-Seattle, 2607 Second Avenue, Seattle, WA 98121-1211.

[Haworth co-indexing entry note]: "A Survey of Factors Contributing to Gay and Lesbian Domestic Violence." Farley, Ned. Co-published simultaneously in *Journal of Gay & Lesbian Social Services* (The Haworth Press, Inc.) Vol. 4, No. 1, 1996, pp. 35-42; and: *Violence in Gay and Lesbian Domestic Partnerships* (ed: Claire M. Renzetti, and Charles Harvey Miley), The Haworth Press, Inc., 1996, pp. 35-42; and: *Violence in Gay and Lesbian Domestic Partnerships* (ed: Claire M. Renzetti, and Charles Harvey Miley) Harrington Park Press, an imprint of The Haworth Press, Inc., 1996, pp. 35-44. Single or multiple copies of this article are available from The Haworth Document Delivery Service [1-800-342-9678, 9:00 a.m. - 5:00 p.m. (EST)].

35

INTRODUCTION

This paper reports on the author's work with gay male and lesbian perpetrators of domestic violence over a six-year period. In 1986, the author began collecting data on both gay and lesbian perpetrators of domestic violence, primarily from screening and intake interviews completed at a counseling agency for sexual minorities and in private practice. The intent was to: (1) explore intergenerational histories of abuse and violence, as well as current involvement in abuse and violence in domestic relationships; and (2) consider connections between addictive/self-abusive behaviors–i.e., secondary abusive behavior–and domestic violence. Preliminary findings were reported in Farley (1985).

HYPOTHESES

Based on subjective clinical experience and perceived emergent patterns from client assessments, the following hypotheses were developed:

1. Gay male and lesbian perpetrators of domestic violence are likely to come from families in which physical and psychological abuse were normative.
2. This pattern of abuse is intergenerational, passed down from the parents of the abusers in this study, with the parents themselves having been abused in their families of origin.
3. Similar to heterosexual perpetrators of domestic violence (Sonkin & Durphy, 1985; Star, 1983), gay and lesbian perpetrators will exhibit a high incidence of addictive/self-abusive behaviors–i.e., secondary abusive behavior–perhaps established as coping mechanisms for the poor self-concepts they had internalized.

METHODS

The methods utilized in this study are qualitative. Thus, the goal was not to provide statistical data that are necessarily representative of all gay/lesbian perpetrators, but rather to offer a subjective under-standing of the experiences of some gay/lesbian perpetrators that may serve as a general profile to guide clinical work.

A total of 288 demographic profiles (males = 119, females = 169) were used. All were clients who had been screened and referred for perpetrator treatment. All 288 clients identified as being in, or as having been in, a same-sex relationship at the time of the domestic violence. These clients completed a domestic violence screening questionnaire and underwent a full psychosocial assessment, inclu-sive of diagnosis using the DSM-III-R.

Data were collected over the six-year period 1986-1991. Clients signed a release of information form that stipulated that nonidenti-fying data would be used for research to secure funding as well as to build a knowledge base.

Data gathered included general demographics (e.g., age, employ-ment, ethno-cultural background, and income), as well as issue-spe-cific information (e.g., substance abuse, addiction to food or sex, legal status, and personal history of physical/sexual/psychological abuse).

FINDINGS

The demographic data are presented in Table 1. As the table indicates, the subjects interviewed came from a broad cross-section of backgrounds within the gay/lesbian community. To summarize, the average subject was in his/her early thirties. Virtually all had completed high school, while a majority had some education be-yond high school. Slightly more gay male subjects were unem-ployed than employed, but considerably more lesbian subjects were unemployed than employed. The modal gross monthly income cate-gory for both gay male and lesbian subjects was $0-$500. The majority of subjects, gay and lesbian, were white, and most were currently involved in an intimate relationship.

The analysis of the psychosocial assessment produced several important findings. Specifically, both men and women reported a high level of previous mental health/psychiatric treatment. Among the men, 87% reported previous mental health treatment, and 27% reported having been hospitalized for psychiatric reasons. Among

TABLE 1. Demographic Data (n = 288; males = 119, females = 169)

Variable	Males	Females
Average age	33.8	31.7
Employment status		
employed full-time	27.0%	25.0%
employed part-time	20.0	12.5
not on the job market	6.0	6.0
unemployed	20.0	12.5
receiving public assistance	27.0	44.0
Gross monthly income		
$0-$500	60.0%	56.0%
$501-$1,000	13.0	25.0
$1,001 or >	27.0	19.0
Highest level of educational attainment		
< 12 years	0.0%	6.0%
12 years	40.0	38.0
13-16 years	53.0	44.0
17 years or >	7.0	12.0
Racial/ethno-cultural background		
White	61.0%	86.0%
African American	13.0	1.0
Hispanic	13.0	6.0
Asian/Pacific Islander	4.0	2.0
Native American	2.0	5.0
Other	7.0	0.0
Relationship status		
currently involved in an intimate relationship	67.0%	81.0%
single or separated	33.0	19.0

the women, 94% reported a mental health treatment history, with 38% having had a psychiatric hospitalization. At the time they were interviewed, 33% of the men and 38% of the women reported being suicidal; 20% of the men and 19% of the women reported being homicidal.

An extensive drug and alcohol screening revealed that 60% of the men and 55.5% of the women did not abuse alcohol or drugs. However, among these substance non-users, many reported compulsive behaviors, particularly around sex and/or food. Of the 288 clients screened, in fact, only 27% of the men and 19% of the women reported no secondary abusive behavior at all.

Diagnostically, primary attention was given to Axis I and Axis II. Diagnostic assessment was conducted by several different clinicians trained in the field. There was no diagnostic category that emerged as applicable to the majority of subjects. Taking into consideration that several subjects had dual diagnoses in both substance abuse and mental health areas, the following results should be considered as primary diagnoses.

Overall, the most common diagnoses were in the Adjustment Disorders (predominantly involving inappropriate conduct), with 20% of the men and 38% of the women receiving such diagnoses. Also prevalent were the Impulse Disorders (particularly Implosive Disorder), with 33% of the men and 19% of the women being diagnosed as such. Thirteen percent of the men and 19% of the women were diagnosed with Affective Disorders; 20% of the men were diagnosed with a Psychotic Disorder, while 7% of the men and 18% of the women were diagnosed with a Personality Disorder that was considered significant (mostly Cluster "B" disorders). Only 7% of the men and 6% of the women received a primary diagnosis of Substance Abuse Disorder.

The final part of the assessment was most directly tied to domestic violence and came from the Domestic Violence Screening form developed by Farley (1985). Here the focus was on personal and historical abuse patterns. *All* of the men and women assessed reported having been psychologically abused as children. For both men and women, childhood experiences of physical abuse (males = 93%, females = 88%) and childhood sexual abuse (males = 67%, females = 94%) also were common. In addition, 67% of the men and 81% of the women reported being psychologically abused as adults, while 53% and 44% of the men and women respectively reported having been physically abused as adults. Adult experiences of sexual abuse were much lower (males = 7%, females = 6%).

In reporting clear knowledge of intergenerational abuse patterns both men (80%) and women (81%) reported that their parents/ guardians were abused as children. It was also found that alcohol abuse was evident in the family of origin for 47% of the men and 44% of the women.

Previous history of being an abuser in adult relationships was high for both men (80%) and women (94%). Finally, because it has become so common for clients to enter treatment utilizing (for better or for worse) the language of the co-dependency movement, it was decided to ask them to rate themselves as predominantly a (1) helper, (2) rescuer, or (3) dependent, in their relationships. Fifty-four percent of the men and 63% of the women reported themselves as dependent.

DISCUSSION

The demographic data show that gay and lesbian batterers come from all segments of the population. They represent all ethnic/racial groups and cut across economic classes, educational backgrounds and occupations.

In terms of the clinical assessments, several provocative findings emerged. It is important to explore some of the possible reasons for these results, including sampling bias and other methodological limitations of the research.

In the area of previous psychiatric hospitalization, the relatively high number of persons reporting previous hospitalizations may simply reflect the type of clients generally seen in the community mental health system, rather than being indicative of the norm among batterers (or among gays/lesbians). Many of the individuals referred for domestic violence treatment to the agency in which this study was conducted (as opposed to the author's private practice) also were referred because of low-income status or psychiatric disability history. In addition, secondary or dual substance abuse/mental health diagnoses may be significant, particularly in light of data showing a higher level of substance abuse within the gay/lesbian population relative to the general population.

With reference to childhood experiences of psychological abuse, the 100% frequency in this sample may be an artifact of how the question was phrased. It may also reflect the tendency among perpetrators to see themselves as victims. It is also important to note that the lower report of psychological abuse victimization as adults and sexual abuse victimization as adults and children among the men may reflect their internalization of culturally-prescribed beliefs about men not being "victims," particularly victims of sexual abuse.

In general, the findings lend support to hypotheses 1 and 2. When one considers the high reported incidence of abuse experienced by the batterers' parents/guardians, one gets a sense of the intergenerational character of abusive behavior. It is important to note as well the high incidence of childhood sexual abuse reported by the batterers in this study.

The author began this study as a means to corroborate his clinical observations. Nevertheless, the high frequency of some reported behaviors and experiences was surprising, particularly the startlingly high incidence of childhood sexual abuse. The relevance of the combination of a history of physical and sexual abuse in the evolution of adult abusive behavior should be the subject of future research.

The study also showed that many adult abusers also are involved in secondary abusive behaviors. The incidence of secondary abusive behavior was high among this sample: 73% of the men and 63% of the women showed some secondary involvement. Although secondary behaviors are not the cause of battering, inhibition is reduced when some substances, especially alcohol or drugs, are used.

The gay/lesbian community has been shown in many studies to have a higher incidence of substance abuse than the general population. The findings reported here are congruent with the extant research, but the additional data with regard to other self-abusive behaviors suggest further ways by which perpetrators may deal with low self-image and insecurity (Miller, 1983). Moreover, by ranking themselves as "dependent," these perpetrators revealed one of the ways they perceive and label themselves as "victims."

CONCLUSION

This study was done over a six-year period in order to recruit a large enough data base from which potentially relevant conclusions might be drawn. Although data similar to those discussed here have been reported in studies of heterosexual male perpetrators (see, for example, Marmor, 1978), this is the first study that has gathered data of this kind from gay/lesbian perpetrators.

This study provides baseline data with respect to gay/lesbian perpetrators of domestic violence. Hopefully, it can be used by the gay/lesbian domestic violence movement to begin to develop strategies for effectively responding to and treating both perpetrators and victims of same-sex domestic violence.

REFERENCES

Farley, N. (1985). *Breaking the myth: An overview of same-sex domestic violence.* Vermont College of Norwich University, Montpelier, VT: Unpublished Manuscript.

Marmor, J. (1978). Psychosocial roots of violence. In R.L. Sadoff (Ed.), *Violence and responsibility* (pp. 7-16). New York: SP Medical and Scientific Books, Spectrum.

Miller, A. (1983). *For your own good: Hidden cruelty in child rearing and the roots of violence.* New York: Hannum.

Sonkin, D.J., & Durphy, M.D. (1985). *Learning to live without violence: A handbook for men.* San Francisco: Volcano Press.

Star, B. (1983). *Helping the abuser.* New York: Family Services Association of America.

PERSONS OF COLOR

Lesbians of Color
and the Domestic Violence Movement

Charlene M. Waldron

SUMMARY. Lesbians of color have been part of the domestic violence movement in a variety of roles. These include survivor, batterer, and service provider. In each of these roles, issues of racism and homophobia have significant impacts on how these women are affected by these roles. Implications for community action are noted. *[Article copies available from The Haworth Document Delivery Service: 1-800-342-9678.]*

Lesbians and women of color have been part of the domestic violence scene even before it became an organized movement. How-

Charlene M. Waldron is an MSW candidate at Boston University School of Social Work. She is a formerly battered Black woman, who worked in the battered women's movement before returning to school. In addition to attending school full-time, she also runs a national grassroots fund raising campaign, and writes and lectures on gay and lesbian domestic violence.

Correspondence may be addressed to the author at 6 Clinton Street, #B, Cambridge, MA 02139-2329.

[Haworth co-indexing entry note]: "Lesbians of Color and the Domestic Violence Movement." Waldron, Charlene M. Co-published simultaneously in *Journal of Gay & Lesbian Social Services* (The Haworth Press, Inc.) Vol. 4, No. 1, 1996, pp. 43-51; and: *Violence in Gay and Lesbian Domestic Partnerships* (ed: Claire M. Renzetti, and Charles Harvey Miley), The Haworth Press, Inc., 1996, pp. 43-51; and: *Violence in Gay and Lesbian Domestic Partnerships* (ed: Claire M. Renzetti, and Charles Harvey Miley) Harrington Park Press, an imprint of The Haworth Press, Inc., 1996, pp. 43-51. Single or multiple copies of this article are available from The Haworth Document Delivery Service [1-800-342-9678, 9:00 a.m. - 5:00 p.m. (EST)].

43

ever, now that the domestic violence movement is beginning to enjoy some media attention and funding, these groups have been marginalized in an effort to garner more public sympathy for the cause. Therefore, the celebrated cases and heroines are white middle-class, straight women. Nevertheless, those of us who work in the movement or who attempt to analyze the problem continue to see that women confronting this issue are far more diverse.

Women of color, lesbians, women of all social classes, and men have been victims of violence. No one is safe from violence. When we accept and understand that violence is a part of our society–that it can be used by or against anyone–we will finally be able to come to grips with this problem so that we may begin to propose solutions (Enos & Rollins, 1988).

It is the inability or refusal to acknowledge that violence can be used by or against anyone that makes it difficult for some people to see lesbians of color as part of the domestic violence movement, other than as service providers. However, as lesbians of color have begun to confront the issue of domestic violence, we have come to see that it is a problem that has implications for us as survivors and as batterers, as well as service providers. The leadership for this work must come from lesbians of color themselves, but white straight women and white lesbians, straight women of color, white gay men and gay men of color are welcome to help and support us, especially in areas in which we are isolated from each other.

In this paper, I will discuss some of the special issues that arise as we simultaneously struggle with sexism, racism, and homophobia within the domestic violence movement as well as the larger society.

LESBIANS OF COLOR AS DOMESTIC VIOLENCE SURVIVORS

The typical battered lesbian experiences a sense of intense isolation. Often, because of a reluctance to identify as lesbian, the battering partner is the only other lesbian with whom the battered lesbian has extensive contact. This means that the battering partner has the opportunity to set the norms for a "typical" lesbian relationship, with the battered lesbian having no others with whom she can engage in a reality check (Hamnontree, 1993; Russo, 1992).

This isolation also contributes to both women in the relationship feeling as if the other is the only person whom they can trust. For the woman being battered this is particularly ironic because although she feels that her partner is the only person whom she can trust, her partner is also the person whom she most fears. The batterer, in turn, may use this "us-against-them" mindset to keep the battered lesbian in the relationship and to reinforce the victim's sense that the consequences to be incurred from going outside the relationship will be far worse than simply remaining silent (West, 1992).

There are, however, a number of ways in which racism can intensify the experience of isolation of the battered lesbian of color. For example, if the batterer is also a woman of color, the batterer may use the prevalence of racism in society to discourage the victim from seeking help. The batterer may also use the community of color to accomplish this same goal by threatening to out the victim in that community, or she may use cultural norms to further oppress the victim. There is an extensive literature that documents the widespread existence of negative and hostile attitudes toward homosexuals within communities of color (see, for example, Clarke, 1983; Hudgins, 1990). However, if the batterer is a white woman, she, too, may use societal racism, as well as the battered lesbian's internalized racism, to keep her partner dependent on her and doubtful of her ability to think and act independently.

The intense isolation characteristic of most abusive relationships may also lead the battered lesbian to attempt to protect her batterer from the rest of the world. The battered lesbian spends so much of her time trying to hide the truth from outsiders, or trying to make herself appear to be the partner with the problem, that she does not have energy left over to take care of herself. It becomes difficult and exhausting for her to seek help. For the battered lesbian of color, however, this problem is exacerbated; besides the energy she must expend to survive in the relationship, the battered lesbian of color must also think not only about what services to get and where to get them, but also whether racism (in addition to sexism and homophobia) will be a barrier to getting the help she needs.

SEEKING HELP FROM SOCIAL SERVICE AGENCIES

One of the first difficulties in seeking and obtaining help that battered lesbians of color confront is access. Although some social service agencies have begun to implement outreach programs for battered lesbians, these may not be successful in reaching battered lesbians of color. For instance, a common means of outreach for such programs is to advertise in local lesbian and gay newspapers. However, this tactic will reach only a small number of battered lesbians of color, since there are many lesbian and bisexual women of color who do not identify themselves as lesbian or bisexual. Such a strategy will also miss the many lesbian and bisexual women of color who may identify as lesbian or bisexual, but whose primary identification is one of color. These women may never read a lesbian or gay newspaper because it is too racist. Finally, this ad may also miss battered lesbian and bisexual women of color because often these women do not identify as battered. If the ad does not explain what battering is, it may be difficult for a woman to recognize that she has been battered. In fact, she will probably identify herself as the batterer if she has fought back in any way. She may also refuse to acknowledge the problem because she does not want to accept any more labels or categories that will force her to deal with more oppression in her life (Stamps, 1992).

Consequently, in order to reach battered lesbians of color, social service agencies must develop outreach strategies that are creative and flexible. This means that rather than simply adding a few words about lesbian relationships to the ads, service providers must think about the specific characteristics and needs of the target population in carefully planning their outreach programs. For instance, rather than advertising only in lesbian and gay newspapers, the agency should consider also advertising in the paper of the community of color, even if it does not have an openly lesbian or gay following. When designing the ad itself, the writers should take care to leave sexual identity open by, for example, using the phrase, "women who have relationships with women," instead of lesbian or bisexual. The ad also should clearly explain battering. This means more than simply noting that domestic violence may be physical, emotional, sexual or psychological. Instead, the ad should provide concrete examples that the average person can understand–e.g., saying, "Your partner forces you to have sex when you don't want to," rather than saying "sexual abuse."

It is also important to be cognizant of the power of networking in communities of color. An important thing to do in an outreach plan is to contact and recruit organizations and leaders in the community of color that have community members' respect and who are used by community members as resources. Often people of color turn to members of their community first for help.

Still, the most important part of any outreach program is the agency's ability to back its efforts. This means having the staff and agency policies in place that will be supportive of and prepared for the target population. It is not good enough for an agency to hire one woman of color to do outreach to all women of color. Moreover, the commitment to a population must start at the highest level–the board of directors–and run throughout the agency. Consequently, there must be lesbians and women of color at all levels of the agency *and* they must also be visible and involved in the agency's day-to-day operations.

Procedures and policies must be in place to address both racism and homophobia. This does not mean some rules written in a book that no one looks at. Rather, the principle that racism and homophobia are unacceptable should be a part of the culture of the agency. The agency should have an ongoing plan on how to deal with issues of racism and homophobia, even when people of color and lesbians are not around to be watchdogs.

At the same time, however, it is wrong to assume that only lesbians of color can work with other lesbians of color. Any caring professional can be helpful if she can be patient and non-judgmental while allowing the client to tell her story in her own way, a way that may involve mistrust, anger and frustration (Hudgins, 1990). The challenge for any service provider working with a battered lesbian of color is not to make the battered lesbian of color responsible for being mindful of racism, sexism, homophobia, and all the other -isms. All workers should be doing the same thing, even if the counselor shares an identity with the battered lesbian of color.

SEEKING HELP FROM THE POLICE

Communities of color and the police have had an uneasy relationship at best for a very long time. Some people of color come from countries where they lived under a police state. Others, like those from the Black community, have watched their people suffer similar atrocities at the hands of police in this country. Gays and lesbians, too, have experienced homophobia and violence by the police. Not surprisingly, therefore, battered lesbians of color may be reluctant to follow advice that involves reporting their abuse to the police for fear of both racism and homophobia from police officers.

When the police are called, they usually are slow to respond and lack sensitivity. Even though police officers are now being trained to respond to domestic violence calls, their attitudes have been slow to change. However, the police are increasingly being called to respond to gay and lesbian domestic violence calls, but they do not appear to be explaining adequately to either victims or batterers the extent of their rights and the consequences of specific actions (Malkin, 1992). For example, survivors are not told that they have a right to get a restraining order or that they have the right to press charges. Similarly, batterers usually are not informed of the seriousness of their actions nor of the legal remedies available to victims.

LESBIANS OF COLOR AS BATTERERS

It is a sad fact that there are some lesbians of color who are batterers. Although it is a touchy subject in the domestic violence movement, women of color cannot afford to ignore the special treatment needs of batterers of color. This is not to say that I personally spend a lot of my energy trying to identify all of the special concerns of batterers. However, as a lesbian of color, I do have some responsibility for maintaining the health and well-being of my community. Thus, if I truly wish to contribute to the effort of developing solutions to domestic violence, I must think about batterers.

When identifying the batterer in a relationship involving a lesbian of color, it is important to be aware of the role that racism may have played in the relationship (Kanuha, 1990a). For example, a white lesbian may say that she feels threatened by her lover when her lover raises her voice; she worries that her lover may get violent. However, after talking with her lover, a lesbian of color, it is discovered that she tends to raise her voice whenever she gets excited, which is normative in her family and her culture, but she does not consider herself violent. In such a situation, the two women may be able to resolve their problem by better understanding each other's cultural norms. It may be the case that the white lesbian has assumed that because a woman of color gets loud, she will naturally get violent.

At the same time, however, we must be careful not to use racism as an excuse for battering. Instead, batterers should be held strictly accountable for choosing to batter. As when dealing with batterers who are alcoholic, it is important for a batterer to be able to identify her own triggers so that she will not be controlled by them.

LESBIANS OF COLOR AS WORKERS IN THE DOMESTIC VIOLENCE MOVEMENT

Lesbians and straight women of color have been working in the domestic violence movement since its inception. However, our contributions and the value of our work to the movement have often been marginalized, viewed as appendices to the "central" work. We and the work we do are often considered expendable when conflicts over budgets and/or ideas arise.

We also are not seen as equals to our white peers. Often, if a woman of color is hired for a job, other workers assume she is less qualified and was only hired as an Affirmative Action "case." These feelings usually are not discussed openly. This may be a result of the misconception that feminists–or at least those in the domestic violence movement–are not racist, or it may be due to the view that the only work of the movement is to deal with the women we serve. In any event, these feelings need to be confronted openly in order to decrease the tension.

Thus far, the battered women's movement has not adequately addressed racism and other forms of oppression within it (Kanuha, 1990b). White women, both straight and lesbian, are afraid that they will be labeled racist, thereby making them partly responsible for the oppression of others. This is a hard pill for them to swallow because they do not want to own up to their power and race privilege. Instead, because of their status as women, they prefer to think of themselves as oppressed, which, in turn, further contributes to the oppression of women of color.

However, women of color, straight and lesbian, also seem afraid to confront these complex issues within the movement. We try to stay focused on white women and what they have done or not done. We fail to look at ourselves and recognize that we participate actively in our oppression through internalized racism (Kanuha, 1990b).

Although a primary purpose of the domestic violence movement is to take care of the needs of battered women, the movement cannot condone the neglect and racist abuse of its own workers. It is widely believed that we should be providing safe and nurturing spaces for the women we serve, but that cannot be done if we do not do the same for ourselves. Consequently, our training should include units on anti-racism for both white women and women of color, as well as anti-homophobia training. We must also provide ourselves safe spaces to talk about these issues as they arise.

LESBIANS OF COLOR AS A COMMUNITY

Although it is important for us to acknowledge that violence is everywhere, it is more important that we not resign ourselves to violence. Lesbians of color must struggle against simple solutions for complex problems. A simple solution, for example, would be to help one woman cope with or improve her situation. A better solution would be to act on a small scale, but to analyze the implications of an individual's situation on our society (Pharr, 1990). Because we sometimes forget that the personal is political, we must remind ourselves.

In addition, lesbians of color cannot forget our need to form alliances with gay men of color. Gay men of color can often help us to identify when racism has played a part in a situation, and it is also good to be able to process what is going on with a group of people to whom one doesn't have to explain racism.

It is important for lesbians of color to be out–not only in the gay community, but also in their community of color. It is also important for lesbians who are not ready to be out to be able to identify lesbians of color as models. We should also work on modeling more healthy relationships among lesbians of color, so that we know what they look like.

However, the most important thing we can do as a community is to talk about the problems. We need to talk about domestic violence in all spaces so that the community becomes more aware of the ramifications of the issue for us. This means talking about how to build healthy relationships, how to get out of bad relationships, what to do with batterers, and similar topics. Knowledge is power, and it is the most effective weapon that we can use against all the -isms that we encounter when addressing this issue.

REFERENCES

Clarke, C. (1983). The failure to transform: Homophobia in the black community. In B. Smith (Ed.), *Home girls: A black feminist anthology* (pp. 197-208). New York: Kitchen Table/Women of Color Press.

Enos, D., & Rollins, C. (1988, February). Lesbian battering: A political analysis. *Matrix*, p. 8.

Hamnontree, M. (1993, December 16). Dark secrets. *Bay Windows*, p. 12.

Hudgins, R. L. (1990). Professional considerations for those working with women of color survivors of lesbian battering. In P. Elliott (Ed.), *Confronting lesbian battering: A manual for the battered women's movement* (pp. 158-160). St. Paul, MN: Lesbian Battering Intervention Project.

Kanuha, V. (1990a). Compounding the triple jeopardy: Battering in lesbian of color relationships. In P. Elliott (Ed.), *Confronting lesbian battering: A manual for the battered women's movement* (pp. 142-157). St. Paul, MN: Lesbian Battering Intervention Project.

Kanuha, V. (1990b). Dealing with conflict in the battered women's movement. In P. Elliott (Ed.), *Confronting lesbian battering: A manual for the battered women's movement* (pp. 21-24). St. Paul, MN: Lesbian Battering Intervention Project.

Malkin, M. (1992, September 3). Oh God, what am I going to do? *Bay Windows*, pp. 3, 13-14.

Pharr, S. (1990). Lesbian battering: Social change urged. In P. Elliott (Ed.), *Confronting lesbian battering: A manual for the battered women's movement* (pp. 19-20). St. Paul, MN: Lesbian Battering Intervention Project.

Russo, A. (1992, May 14). A battered lesbian fights for recognition. *Sojourner*, pp. 16-17.

Stamps, W. (1992, July/August). Betrayal of passion. *On Our Backs*, pp. 31-35.

West, A. (1992). Prosecutorial activism: Confronting heterosexism in a lesbian battering case. *Harvard Women's Law Journal, 15*, 249-271.

White, E. C. (1985). *Chain, chain, change: For black women dealing with physical and emotional abuse*. Seattle, WA: Seal Press.

Serving Gays and Lesbians of Color
Who Are Survivors of Domestic Violence

Juan M. Méndez

SUMMARY. People who provide services to gay and lesbian survivors of domestic violence must reflect the diversity of the communities they serve. Strategies to diversify services may include the volunteer recruitment process. People of color should be represented among staff who do advocacy, run support groups, and provide interpretation services for survivors. Knowledge of immigration issues is essential for effective services to a diverse population, as well as awareness of how racism acts as a barrier to an effective response of the criminal justice system to gays and lesbians of color. *[Article copies available from The Haworth Document Delivery Service: 1-800-342-9678.]*

This paper is based largely on my experiences at the New York City Gay and Lesbian Anti-Violence Project. As domestic violence

Juan M. Méndez, BBA, is Domestic Violence Coordinator at the New York City Gay and Lesbian Anti-Violence Project.

This paper is based on a presentation delivered as part of a panel on underserved populations at the Domestic Violence Pre-Conference Institute of the National Lesbian and Gay Health Conference, June, 1994, in New York. It has been edited slightly for publication.

Correspondence may be addressed to the author at the New York City Gay and Lesbian Anti-Violence Project, 647 Hudson, New York, NY 10014.

[Haworth co-indexing entry note]: "Serving Gays and Lesbians of Color Who Are Survivors of Domestic Violence." Méndez, Juan M. Co-published simultaneously in *Journal of Gay & Lesbian Social Services* (The Haworth Press, Inc.) Vol. 4, No. 1, 1996, pp. 53-59; and: *Violence in Gay and Lesbian Domestic Partnerships* (ed: Claire M. Renzetti, and Charles Harvey Miley), The Haworth Press, Inc., 1996, pp. 53-59; and: *Violence in Gay and Lesbian Domestic Partnerships* (ed: Claire M. Renzetti, and Charles Harvey Miley) Harrington Park Press, an imprint of The Haworth Press, Inc., 1996, pp. 53-59. Single or multiple copies of this article are available from The Haworth Document Delivery Service [1-800-342-9678, 9:00 a.m. - 5:00 p.m. (EST)].

53

coordinator at the AVP, I have tried not only to diversify services, but also to diversify the client population whom we have been serving.[1]

Let me begin by first stating what to some may be the obvious. Specifically, if one wants to serve a diverse population, then one's staff, or the people who are going to provide direct service, must reflect the characteristics of the population one aims to serve. Of course, many programs, such as the domestic violence project at AVP, have only one full-time staff member. Nevertheless, most also have a number of volunteers or peer counselors who also offer client services. Those positions should be diversified if one wants to be inclusive and serve a diverse population.

For example, in order to increase our Latino population, we focused on our subway campaign, which originally appeared in 1991. The campaign featured a subway poster on which appeared a picture of an extended hand and the text, "If your lesbian or gay partner is using one of these to hurt you, we have one to help you." In October 1993, when we decided to repeat this campaign, we also decided to include a Spanish version of the poster, realizing that this would likely increase the number of Spanish-speaking callers to our hotline.

To be prepared for this response, we wanted to increase the number of Spanish-speaking volunteers staffing the hotline *before* we put up the poster. To do this, we tried an approach to volunteer recruitment that on its face seemed logical, but which in practice did not work. Specifically, we went to the gay and lesbian people of color groups that meet at the Lesbian and Gay Community Center and we tried to persuade them to be hotline volunteers at AVP. This experience taught us that these people already have a commitment to the community through the groups in which they are involved; most are not in a position to overextend themselves by taking on the responsibility of being trained as a hotline counselor while at the same time remaining active in their other organizations.

Consequently, as an alternative, we tried a riskier strategy: we went mainstream by placing an ad in the Spanish paper *El Diario-La Prensa,* which is not a gay paper. Our ad appeared in the community calendar section where listings are free and was composed of two paragraphs asking for volunteers for a gay and lesbian counseling line. The response to this ad was overwhelming; we had people calling non-stop for two weeks offering to volunteer. Although some of the callers were not appropriate for the job,[2] many were and, surprisingly, these were Latino gay men and lesbians who had no previous knowledge about the Lesbian and Gay Community Center in New York and who were not involved in a Latino gay and lesbian organization or any other people of color organization at the time. Their only involvement in the community was in terms of socializing in the bars and clubs, and they wanted to do something more. The way they found they could get involved was through their local Spanish-language newspaper. As a result, AVP was able to recruit 12 new volunteers, increasing the total number of bilingual volunteers to 14.

Issues of diversity should also be taken into consideration with respect to those people who will provide advocacy services to gay and lesbian survivors of domestic violence, those who will accompany a client to a hospital or a police precinct, and those who will help a client request an order for protection. In some cases, for instance, these helpers will have to interpret or translate services for clients who are not native English speakers.

Another area in need of culturally diverse strategies is support groups. At AVP, for example, we are in the process of putting together a Latina/Latino domestic violence support group, which also is going to be co-gender. This is being done at AVP for the first time, and I am unaware of any other agency which previously has tried it. To do this, we met with two social workers–a Latina lesbian and a Latino gay man–and we agreed that in Latino culture, lesbians and gay men tend not to be as separatist as non-Latinos are in terms of gender.[3] In being cognizant of this cultural difference and applying it to a support group modality, we are hoping to be more effective in our outreach to Latina lesbian and Latino gay male victims of domestic violence.

Many service providers recognize the obvious need for the availability of multi-language materials. However, when attempting to translate materials that were first written in English, it is important to remember that one should not hire a consultant who is a translator exclusively, but rather one who is also an interpreter–that is, one who can rewrite the information in a culturally-appropriate, as well as an accurate, manner. For example, if the syntax of a particular statement is translated literally from English to any other language without being checked for interpretation, the meaning of the original thought may be altered significantly.

One must also recognize that within the Latino population, as well as other people of color populations, there are likely to be individuals who also will need advocacy for immigration-related issues. For instance, a number of our clients at AVP are not documented and come from countries where homosexuality is strongly prosecuted and people "disappear" simply because they are gay. In these countries, gays often are picked up by the police and later are found dead in a mass grave. For obvious reasons, individuals from these countries are going to experience tremendous difficulty reporting domestic violence to the police. Advocates must recognize that they will need to provide such clients with much information, and that it will take a great deal of work and patience to see the client through this process. Moreover, service providers must reassure the client that they will be with him or her throughout the entire process.

An important point for advocates in these situations to remember is that many batterers use the undocumented status of the victim as another weapon of power and control. They might say, for instance, "If you don't do what I say, if you dare leave me, if you report this to the police, I'm going to call INS [the Immigration and Naturalization Service], and 'they' are going to come in the van and pick you up." In New York City, this is a hollow threat due to an executive order (EO#124, signed by Mayor Koch in 1989) that mandates all city agencies not to request or take into consideration immigration-related information or make any type of report to INS. However, even in New York, many survivors have no knowledge of the executive order and are terrified of going to the police, or even to a hospital or an emergency room to get medical care, because they think this information is going to be requested as part of intake. It is important for service providers to be aware of their local statutes regarding immigration status and to educate their communities about them.[4]

A related issue with all clients of color who are survivors of domestic violence is how to help them see the police as a helpful resource. There is a well-justified mistrust of the police within communities of color, stemming largely from the long history of police brutality and racism against communities of color. Nevertheless, clients should look to the police for a response to their calls for help, and service providers should do as much as they can to make the legal system work for clients.

I wish to close this paper with a brief story. In December, 1993, the New York *Daily News* published a one-page article about domestic violence in gay and lesbian relationships. For the article, news staff wanted to interview a survivor and maybe even publish his or her picture. Not surprisingly, it was difficult to find survivors who were willing to be interviewed, but two men did volunteer on condition that they could do so anonymously. Subsequently, another survivor, an African-American gay man who was almost murdered by his batterer, decided to go public; he did not want other people to go through what he had experienced, and he wanted to let others know about this problem.[5] He was interviewed for the article, and his picture was taken and published.

The article itself was well-written; it was sensitive to the issue and to the victims. However, the title of the article–selected by the editor, not the writer–was the opposite. The article was entitled, "Gays can bash each other, too" (Furse, 1993). The title presents two problems. First, it used the term "bash," which is a term used to describe homophobic violence against lesbians and gay men. Second, the title implies that there is some sort of mutuality in cases of gay and lesbian domestic violence.

Although the article was accurate and sensitively written, the staff at AVP wrote a letter to the editor of the paper to register our protest about the article's title. Meanwhile, the client, David, who was interviewed for the article and whose picture appeared with it, received some flack from his relatives for doing the article–mostly because he came out as a gay man. At the same time, however, David also got a supportive response from his friends, and we at AVP received a call from an African-American gay group. The group did not want us to do a training or formal presentation for them on this topic, but rather wished to discuss the topic amongst themselves, utilizing statistics and other information provided by our program. Based on a follow-up call I received from one of the organizers, the outcome was successful; many of those attending shared their stories as survivors of abusive relationships, thus breaking the silence on the subject for this community.

I have related this experience because it illustrates the importance of service providers offering information to members of communities of color so that a dialogue about same-sex domestic violence within these communities may begin. Our job as service providers to gay and lesbian victims of domestic violence is to put out the message that domestic violence happens in all segments of our community, regardless of race, ethnicity, class, age, ability, politics, or religion. We must be certain that our message and our services reach every one of these diverse segments that make up our lesbian and gay communities if we are to help all those who are victimized become survivors.

NOTES

1. A number of the issues raised in this paper have been taken up in forums such as the National Gay and Lesbian Task Force People of Color Institute; the Diversity Institute; and the Race, Class, and Gender Institute. However, I am applying these issues here specifically to the problem of domestic violence.

2. As is the case in any volunteer recruitment, we often have people approach us who might have a mental health issue or problem. In addition, our goal was to recruit volunteers who were gay and lesbian identified. Therefore, when a candidate phoned to volunteer, we asked him or her to come in for an interview so we could do an assessment. This proved to be a valuable process, since during the interviews issues sometimes arose that indicated that the candidate was not appropriate for the position. For example, if during a discussion of domestic violence, the candidate indicated that he or she did not perceive this to be a problem, or justified or minimized it, he or she was not considered appropriate for the volunteer training.

3. This was something that I personally was aware of before I moved to New York from Puerto Rico. In Puerto Rico, there is no such thing as a gay male bar or a lesbian bar. There are bars that may be frequented more by lesbians than gay men, and vice versa, but in terms of socializing, everyone was welcome.

4. It is also the case that INS generally is not interested in individual reports of people who are undocumented. Victims should be advised to ignore any batterer who calls INS on the phone to make such a report. INS simply does not have the resources or capacity to keep track of individual reports and follow them up. The exception, however, would be any individual who is HIV-positive, since there is a ban on the entry of HIV-positive individuals into this country (Burris, 1993). Such clients should be advised that INS will probably look closely at these kinds of reports.

5. In this case, the police response had been effective, but this was likely because they literally had a trail of blood to follow from the apartment to the public phone, where the victim had called 911 and then passed out. The case went to court, and we were lucky to have a good prosecuting attorney who took the case seriously and decided to ask for the maximum sentence of 25 years to life in prison. The batterer pleaded guilty before going to trial and was sentenced to 20 years to life in prison.

REFERENCES

Burris, S. (Ed.). (1993). *AIDS law today: A new guide for the public.* New Haven: Yale University Press.

Furse, J. (1993, December 5). Gays bash each other, too. *New York Daily News,* p. 46.

The Poverty of Services
for Battered Lesbians

Claire M. Renzetti

SUMMARY. This paper addresses the poverty of services available to lesbian victims of partner abuse, despite the need for such services. Drawing on data from a survey of 1,505 help providers (to which 566 responded), the paper focuses on the services that the help providers themselves claim to offer. The data reveal a serious disparity in help providers' rhetoric and official policies and the reality of

Claire M. Renzetti, PhD, is Chairperson and Professor of Sociology at St. Joseph's University.

Dr. Renzetti wishes to thank Mary Allen at the Minnesota Coalition for Battered Women; Pam Elliott at Alternatives in St. Paul, MN; and Lynn Thompson-Haas at the Austin Rape Crisis Center. The work these women shared with the author provided the framework for the questionnaire used to collect the data discussed in this paper. The financial assistance of the Board on Faculty Research at St. Joseph's University also is gratefully acknowledged.

Correspondence may be addressed to the author at Department of Sociology, St. Joseph's University, 5600 City Avenue, Philadelphia, PA 19131.

[Haworth co-indexing entry note]: "The Poverty of Services for Battered Lesbians." Renzetti, Claire M. Co-published simultaneously in *Journal of Gay & Lesbian Social Services* (The Haworth Press, Inc.) Vol. 4, No. 1, 1996, pp. 61-68; and: *Violence in Gay and Lesbian Domestic Partnerships* (ed: Claire M. Renzetti, and Charles Harvey Miley), The Haworth Press, Inc., 1996, pp. 61-68; and: *Violence in Gay and Lesbian Domestic Partnerships* (ed: Claire M. Renzetti, and Charles Harvey Miley) Harrington Park Press, an imprint of The Haworth Press, Inc., 1996, pp. 61-68. Single or multiple copies of this article are available from The Haworth Document Delivery Service [1-800-342-9678, 9:00 a.m. - 5:00 p.m. (EST)].

the services available. The paper concludes with suggestions for improving services to battered lesbians. *[Article copies available from The Haworth Document Delivery Service: 1-800-342-9678.]*

INTRODUCTION

The decision to leave an abusive relationship typically is mediated by the availability of alternative options and resources. Recognition of this fact has been a major contributing factor to the opening of domestic violence agencies, organizations, and shelters for battered heterosexual women and their children. Unfortunately, such services are not readily available to battered lesbians–or at least battered lesbians do not appear to consider them feasible sources of help–despite recent research that documents a need for these services (see, for example, Renzetti, 1992a; Lie, Schilit, Bush, Montagne, & Reyes, 1991; Coleman, 1990; Loulan, 1987). Indeed, in a survey of 100 self-identified battered lesbians (Renzetti, 1992a), the majority of the study participants indicated that they had not sought help from domestic violence hotlines, shelters, and similar agencies because they perceived these services to be for battered heterosexual women only. They expected to be turned away or made to feel uncomfortable by these help providers simply because they are lesbians.

To what extent are these perceptions accurate? In an effort to answer that question, a survey of 1,505 service providers listed in the *1991 National Directory of Domestic Violence Programs* compiled by the National Coalition Against Domestic Violence was undertaken in September, 1991.[1] By the spring of 1992, 566 questionnaires (38%) had been completed and returned.[2] The present paper discusses the results of that survey, looking first at help providers' official policies, then at their reports of the services they actually offer to battered lesbians. Although no direct evidence of the quality of these services is available, the data do allow us to make some cautious inferences about the issue of quality. Finally, the paper concludes with suggestions for improving services to battered lesbians.

HOW TO DISCRIMINATE AGAINST BATTERED LESBIANS WITHOUT REALLY TRYING: POLICIES VERSUS REALITIES

One of the first questions asked of service providers in the survey under discussion here was, "Does your service welcome lesbians as clients?" Ninety-six percent of the respondents answered this question affirmatively. Importantly, however, when asked to describe specifically how they make it clear that lesbians are welcome, 90 service providers (16.5% of 544) did not respond, i.e., they left the space provided for their answers blank. The majority indicated that their organizations adhere to an Affirmative Action/nondiscrimination policy; typical were the following responses:

Volunteers are trained to care for the people involved, not to question lifestyles.

Standard "non-discrimination" clauses in all our materials.

We do not say, "All lesbians we are here for you," just as we do not say, "All female wives of male husbands we are here for you."

An additional 73 service providers (13.4% of 544) gave more vague responses, such as:

We try to remain open and aware.

We encourage diversity.

By being open and honest.

We won't turn them away.

A number of respondents in this group also claimed that the mere presence of lesbians on their staff indicates to lesbian victims that they are welcome at that organization or agency.[3] Several others wrote "through word of mouth in the community," or "by word of mouth from lesbians we have served." Twenty-two service providers felt that the display of lesbian posters, artwork, and literature in their offices should indicate to lesbian victims that they are welcome.

Clearly, for most service providers, the notion of "welcoming" lesbian victims as clients has a rather broad meaning. Indeed, only 53 service providers (9.7% of 544) reported efforts that were specifically designed for lesbian victims. These included distributing brochures on lesbian battering, advertising services in local lesbian/gay newspapers and other media, and offering support groups for battered lesbians.

The disparity between service providers' rhetoric and the actual availability of services for battered lesbians is underlined by additional survey results. For example, although the majority of respondents (77.4%) stated that the written materials compiled and distributed by their agencies or organizations use inclusive language (rather than sex-specific pronouns) to refer to battering victims and batterers, only 25.8% reported that these written materials explicitly address the issue of lesbian battering. Only 29.5% even have brochures or other written materials available that focus exclusively on lesbian battering.

Similarly, two-thirds (66.3%) of the service providers who responded stated that staff at their organizations and agencies receive anti-homophobia training, but less than half (47.9%) indicated that staff receive training specifically on lesbian battering. More disturbing are the findings with respect to volunteer training, since most domestic violence agencies and organizations have small staffs and rely heavily on volunteers, who have the greatest direct interaction with clients. Of the 527 organizations that utilized volunteers, 56.2% reported that their volunteers receive anti-homophobia training; just 40.6% reported that their volunteers receive training specifically on lesbian battering.

Recent research has vividly documented the homophobia rampant in our contemporary society (see, for example, Herek & Berrill, 1992). Anti-homophobia training has been instrumental in illuminating this prejudice and discrimination—even among individuals and groups who consider themselves "politically correct" and who claim to harbor no negative stereotypes about lesbians and gay men. Consequently, the question arises as to how an agency or organization can claim to "welcome" lesbians as clients when they have not taken the time to examine the issues of individual and institutionalized homophobia? Moreover, what is the quality of the services they can provide without such an examination and in light of the fact that so few of those who work most directly with clients are educated about lesbian battering?

It may be argued that the rather casual, sometimes flippant, attitude toward battered lesbians that respondents to this survey often expressed is a reflection of the homophobia they have left unaddressed. Homophobia, though, comes in many forms and, even if individuals within these agencies and organizations are not themselves homophobic, they may be reluctant to provide specific services to lesbian victims or they may conceal the services they do provide because they are afraid of losing funding (Irvine, 1990; Renzetti, 1992a). In other words, their attitudes and behavior are reactions to the homophobia of public and private funding sources.

Another reason that service providers give for not offering more services specifically for lesbian victims is that there have been few or no requests for such services. When asked what percentage of the requests they get for help come from lesbian victims, 12.7% of the respondents said 0, 43.3% said 1 or 2, 27.5% said 10 or less, and only 2.4% reported more than 10%. Virtually all of the respondents (93.1%) indicated that these numbers were estimates, so it is impossible to determine their accuracy. However, in light of their answers to earlier items on the survey, a chicken-and-egg type of question arises: Does the lack of services (and the apparent poor quality of the services that are available) reflect lack of need, or are lesbians not requesting help from these agencies and organizations because they don't think the help will be forthcoming or beneficial? As noted at the outset of this paper, recent research indicates that the latter is most likely correct, and the responses of the help providers to this survey reveal that battered lesbians' negative perceptions of most domestic violence service organizations and agencies are not without foundation.

Although most of the service providers surveyed reported that they had no plans to expand their services for battered lesbians, 32.5% (184) indicated that such plans were underway or that "if the need arises" or "funding can be secured," they would like to expand their services for battered lesbians. When asked to describe their expansion plans, typical responses included improving outreach to the lesbian community, starting support groups for battered lesbians, and incorporating information about lesbian battering into staff and/or volunteer training. How can such services be made truly welcoming to battered lesbians?

IMPROVING SERVICES FOR BATTERED LESBIANS

As I have written elsewhere (Renzetti, 1992b), if domestic violence agencies and organizations maintain that their doors are open to battered lesbians, they must make good on that claim. This involves more than simply posting a non-discrimination statement. First and foremost, it means recognizing and overcoming homophobia within the agency or organization and within oneself. As Elliott (1990, n.p.) has written, "Before you . . . can acknowledge lesbian battering, you must first acknowledge lesbian relationships."

Among the resources available to service providers for this purpose perhaps the best are *Confronting Homophobia* and *Confronting Lesbian Battering,* edited by Guth and Elliott (1990) for the Lesbian Advocacy Committee of the Minnesota Coalition for Battered Women. The first manual contains training materials, suggestions for workshops, sample training formats, and training evaluation forms. The second is a collection of articles and other materials that address the many myths commonly held about lesbian battering and that sensitively challenge readers to reconsider traditional models of intimate violence.

Confronting Lesbian Battering also contains a list of suggestions for making battered women's programs more accessible to battered lesbians (pp. 79-80) as well as a series of questions to assist help providers in knowing if they are ready to work with battered women who are lesbians (pp. 77-78). In reading through these materials one gets a very clear sense of what is needed to make domestic violence services truly welcoming to battered lesbians: the explicit recognition of lesbian battering as a serious problem; non-homophobic staff and volunteers who have been trained specifically about lesbian battering; explicit policies for addressing homophobia among staff, volunteers, and heterosexual clients; written and spoken language that is not heterosexist; materials that are gender neutral and inclusive of lesbian and gay relationships; programming, advertising, community education, and media campaigns specifically on lesbian battering.

The problem of violence in lesbian relationships will not go away by ignoring it or by continuing to deny that it exists. And battered lesbians will not be helped by agencies and organizations who simply pay lip service to non-discrimination policies. Indeed, the unresponsiveness of most service providers to the needs of battered lesbians helps to perpetuate the problem of lesbian battering by leaving batterers unaccountable and jeopardizing the safety of nonviolent lesbians.

NOTES

1. It is worth noting that the NCADV directory provides a "profile of services" for each organization listed that includes information such as whether the service is wheelchair accessible, whether services for the deaf are available, and what languages other than English are spoken. *Not* included is information about whether services specifically designed to address the needs of battered lesbians are available. NCADV, however, does publish a brochure on violence in lesbian relationships.

2. An earlier discussion of this study (Renzetti, 1992b) was based on the preliminary analysis of 557 completed questionnaires. It should also be noted that there appeared to be a good dispersion in terms of the geographic location of the service providers who responded: 19.4% were located in the northeastern United States, 24.6% were in the Midwest, 17.3% were in the south, 8.1% were in the southwest, and 16.3% were in the west. However, geographic location could not be determined for 14.3% of the respondents.

3. A recent study of 100 self-identified battered lesbians (Renzetti, 1992a) casts some doubt on this assumption. A number of the women in this study worked at domestic violence shelters and agencies, but did not perceive them to be sources of help for dealing with their own problems. More disturbing was the finding that four of the women could not go to their local shelters for help because their abusers worked there.

REFERENCES

Coleman, V.E. (1990). *Violence between lesbian couples: A between groups comparison.* Unpublished doctoral dissertation. University Microfilms International, 9109022.

Elliott, P. (Ed.). (1990). *Confronting lesbian battering.* St. Paul: Minnesota Coalition for Battered Women.

Guth, J., & Elliott, P. (Eds.). (1990). *Confronting homophobia*. St. Paul: Minnesota Coalition for Battered Women.

Herek, G., & Berrill, K. (Eds.). (1992). *Hate crimes*. Newbury Park, CA: Sage.

Irvine, J. (1990). Lesbian battering: The search for shelter. In P. Elliott (Ed.), *Confronting lesbian battering* (pp. 25-30). St. Paul: Minnesota Coalition for Battered Women.

Lie, G., Schilit, R., Bush, J., Montagne, M., & Reyes, L. (1991). Lesbians in currently aggressive relationships: How frequently do they report aggressive past relationships? *Violence and Victims, 6,* 121-135.

Loulan, J. (1987). *Lesbian passion*. San Francisco: Spinsters/Aunt Lute.

Renzetti, C.M. (1992a). *Violent betrayal: Partner abuse in lesbian relationships*. Newbury Park, CA: Sage.

Renzetti, C.M. (1992b, May). Services for battered lesbians: Service providers' claims vs. the realities. *Gay and Lesbian Domestic Violence Newsletter, 2,* 1-2.

Twin Epidemics:
Domestic Violence and HIV Infection Among Gay and Bisexual Men

Patrick Letellier

SUMMARY. Gay and bisexual male victims of domestic violence present social service providers with a complex array of problems related to their being both battered and, in many cases, affected by HIV disease. Service providers need to be aware of the issues these men face and be able to help them cope with both epidemics. Accepting a man's victimization as real, regardless of the size, weight, and health status of his partner is a necessary first step. Understanding that HIV does not cause battering but can be an ominous weapon of control is crucial. It is also necessary to understand the impact that HIV has on a man's decision to remain with or leave his violent partner; a decision that may differ given the particular HIV status of the victim and/or his battering partner. *[Article copies available from The Haworth Document Delivery Service: 1-800-342-9678.]*

Patrick Letellier, MA, is Case Manager of the Family Violence Project in the San Francisco District Attorney's Office. He is a member of the Advisory Committee to the Gay Men's Domestic Violence Project at Community United Against Violence. He has written and presented numerous papers on domestic violence, and is co-author of the book *Men who beat the men who love them: Battered gay men and domestic violence.* Mr. Letellier is also a survivor of gay domestic violence.

Correspondence may be addressed to the author at Community United Against Violence, 973 Market Street, Suite 500, San Francisco, CA 94103.

[Haworth co-indexing entry note]: "Twin Epidemics: Domestic Violence and HIV Infection Among Gay and Bisexual Men." Letellier, Patrick. Co-published simultaneously in *Journal of Gay & Lesbian Social Services* (The Haworth Press, Inc.) Vol. 4, No. 1, 1996, pp. 69-81; and: *Violence in Gay and Lesbian Domestic Partnerships* (ed: Claire M. Renzetti, and Charles Harvey Miley), The Haworth Press, Inc., 1996, pp. 69-81; and: *Violence in Gay and Lesbian Domestic Partnerships* (ed: Claire M. Renzetti, and Charles Harvey Miley) Harrington Park Press, an imprint of The Haworth Press, Inc., 1996, pp. 69-81. Single or multiple copies of this article are available from The Haworth Document Delivery Service [1-800-342-9678, 9:00 a.m. - 5:00 p.m. (EST)].

69

Experts in the field of domestic violence estimate that violence in same-sex relationships occurs at approximately the same rate as in heterosexual relationships (Island & Letellier, 1991; Lobel, 1986). That is, about one in five men in an intimate relationship with another man will be battered. In terms of actual numbers, Island and Letellier (1991) estimate that approximately 500,000 gay men will be victims of partner violence each year. This figure, however, may be low, particularly given that the Seattle Counseling Service for Sexual Minorities estimates that every year 30,000 gay men are battered in Seattle alone (Farley, 1990). While precise figures are elusive in the absence of reliable prevalence studies, what is known is that gay and bisexual men are being abused and battered by their partners in startlingly high numbers.

Unlike gay domestic violence, which has been universally ignored as a health problem by the gay community (Szymanski, 1991; Tuller, 1994), HIV and its impact on gay and bisexual men have been closely monitored. In San Francisco, of the 28,000 people infected with HIV, 86% are known to be men who have sex with men (San Francisco Department of Public Health, 1994). While San Francisco is indeed one of the epicenters of AIDS in the United States, HIV infection rates among gay and bisexual men nationally are equally alarming. Of the estimated one million Americans currently infected with HIV, 62% are gay and bisexual men (Centers for Disease Control, 1993). Gay and bisexual men currently account for 58% of the AIDS cases in this country (CDC, 1993), and as many as 30-40% of those men are in committed, primary relationships (Barrett, 1993; Harry & Duvall, 1978).

These statistics and figures point to a sizable minority of gay and bisexual men who must contend with *both* HIV infection and partner abuse as part of their daily lives. The intersection of these two epidemics is clearly visible at the Gay Men's Domestic Violence Project in San Francisco, where 30% of the battered gay and bisexual men to whom the project provides services are HIV-positive (Merrill, personal communication, 1994).

The purpose of this article is to explore some of the difficulties and complexities gay and bisexual men face as they confront the two potentially lethal epidemics of HIV infection and domestic violence in the context of their intimate relationships. First, it will be argued that HIV infection does not cause domestic violence. I will also examine HIV as a weapon of control and the impact of HIV infection on the ability of a battered man to leave his violent partner. Social service providers must be able to understand HIV infection in the context of partner abuse, and vice versa, in order to provide the appropriate support and intervention that battered gay and bisexual men need. Therefore, suggestions and guidelines for these helpers will be included throughout this article. It is hoped that this article and the others in this volume will help service providers, members of the gay, lesbian and bisexual community, and workers in the heterosexual domestic violence movement to appreciate the complexity of same-sex battering, and to understand the dire need for a community-wide response to help stop the violence.

HIV INFECTION DOES NOT CAUSE BATTERING

While there is considerable controversy in the literature and the domestic violence movement about the etiology of battering, such as whether battering is sociopolitically, gender and/or psychologically based (see Merrill, this volume), there is universal agreement that perpetrators choose to be violent (Caesar & Hamberger, 1989; Frank & Houghton, 1987; Sonkin & Durphy, 1989). Though it may seem to a victim that his battering lover is wildly "out of control," batterer behavior is always intentional and deliberate (Gondolf, 1985). Battering is not a matter of losing control over one's behavior; rather, it is a systematic and deliberate pattern of abuse used to gain control over one's partner. As Frank and Houghton (1987) explain, batterers give themselves permission to be violent. The abuse is chosen, and other behavioral choices are always available.

To attribute a perpetrator's violence to any outside cause or force is to excuse the violence or blur the responsibility for its occurrence. For example, alcohol or other substance abuse does not cause battering; nor does job stress, poverty, anger, an abusive childhood, or a "bad day." HIV and AIDS also do not cause domestic violence. HIV and its attendant illnesses can create harrowing experiences in the lives of gay and bisexual men with this disease and for their caregiving partners. Indeed, "the characteristics of AIDS place it among the most stressful diseases for the caregiver: it is unpredictable, its symptoms are difficult to manage, and it produces debilitating and/or disfiguring effects" (Folkman, Chesney, & Christopher-Richards, 1993, p. 4). Nonetheless, HIV does not produce, cause, or in any way justify abuse and violence. However, many gay and bisexual men who are assaulted by their partners are quick to attribute the violence to the stress their partners may be under as a result of health problems related to HIV that one or both are suffering. As one gay man who had been assaulted by his partner explained to the author, "He is not usually like this, really. He's just freaked because he may not be able to go back to work after this [bout of illness]."

When working with battered gay and bisexual men it is important not to label HIV as the culprit responsible for the violence. Accurate information about the dynamics of power and control in relationships where battering occurs can help victims of domestic violence see the violence as part of a larger relationship dynamic rather than as a specific response to some health-related problem. Gay and bisexual men who credit their partner's violence to HIV can also be reminded that the vast majority of people with HIV and AIDS, and their caregivers, do not abuse their partners. Helpers must reiterate to their clients that no matter how stressful AIDS can be, partner abuse is not an appropriate coping strategy.

HIV AS A WEAPON OF CONTROL

Perpetrators of domestic violence report that they use physical violence against their partners because it is a highly effective means of control (Sinclair, 1990). Physical violence, however, is but one means of coercion, and perpetrators will use whatever is available to them to dominate and control their partners. While most literature on batterers' coercive behavior is based on studies of heterosexual men, recent research on lesbian battering demonstrates that lesbian batterers, too, display a terrifying ingenuity in their selection of abusive tactics, frequently tailoring the abuse to the specific vulnerabilities of their partner (Renzetti, 1992). Abusive gay and bisexual men are likely to be equally ingenious in choosing their weapons of control, and HIV can be a very powerful weapon.

Battered gay and bisexual men are clearly at high risk for HIV infection. Rape and sexual assault are often an integral part of a perpetrator's violence (Browne, 1987; Renzetti, 1992; Russell, 1982), and there is little reason to believe that a man who will rape his partner will only do so using a condom. A man who will beat and/or sexually abuse his partner is not likely to care enough to protect him from HIV infection. From the victim's perspective, conversations about safe sex or insistence on condom use may become "triggers" for violence (Jacob, 1993), such that resisting unsafe sex may mean a physical battering in addition to a sexual assault. As one battered women's advocate points out, "Women who are getting beat up don't have the option of using condoms" (Jacob, 1993, p. 24). Obviously, this is equally true for battered gay and bisexual men.

Perhaps even more insidious is the perpetrator who deliberately infects his partner with HIV so as to keep the man from leaving. The perpetrator may reason that infecting his partner makes his partner less desirable to others and more dependent on him and the relationship. As one HIV-positive heterosexual batterer put it, after infecting his partner, "If I can't have you, then no one can. Now you have to stay with me" (quoted in Jacob, 1993, p. 24).

Regardless of the motivation for the infection, battered gay and bisexual men are at high risk, and social service providers need to talk about HIV infection and sexual assault with their clients. Accurate information about safe sex should be made available to these men, as their partners may be insisting that unsafe sex practices are actually safe. Helpers must not assume that all gay and bisexual men know what constitutes safe sex. Battered men are likely to be extremely isolated from the gay community and thereby unable to obtain accurate information about safe sex practices. Furthermore, much of the literature on AIDS and safe sex has targeted white, middle-class gay and bisexual men, leaving gay men of color, low-income gay men, and gay youth particularly vulnerable to infection (Peterson & Marin, 1988; *San Francisco Sentinel*, 1994). Frank discussions about sexual behaviors and potential HIV infection must become part of domestic violence interventions that are initiated by service providers.

Although actual infection may be the most devastating use of HIV by a perpetrator against his partner, threats concerning HIV are also powerful mechanisms of control and need to be taken seriously. Threats to infect with HIV, threats to withhold medicine or not allow a man to seek medical attention, and threats to reveal HIV-positive status are but a few of the tactics used by abusers to create an atmosphere of intimidation and fear that can immobilize their partners. Threats against battered HIV-positive men may be especially effective in maintaining a batterer's control, since having their sexual orientation and/or serostatus made public could result in job loss and the subsequent loss of health insurance, in addition to other forms of anti-gay or AIDS discrimination (Schulman, 1991).

Service providers need to understand the various forms, as well as the magnitude, of AIDS discrimination in this country and address the fears of battered men facing such threats. Like other victims of domestic violence, battered men are best helped when they are made aware of their options and encouraged to make decisions for themselves about what is best for them. Focusing on the victim's physical and emotional safety is always a top priority. For some men, access to information about their legal rights where HIV is concerned may be particularly useful.

NOT "REAL" OR "WORTHY" VICTIMS

A major problem confronting battered gay and bisexual men is the inability or unwillingness of other people to accept their victimization as legitimate. From a variety of different and influential sources, these men often get the clear message that they are not "real" victims, despite the violence they experienced.

Many battered gay and bisexual men report that when they told friends, co-workers, or family members about their partner's violence, they were criticized for not "standing up" for themselves, fighting back, or learning to "take it like a man" (Island & Letellier, 1991). Conversely, when victims respond to their partners' attack with violence of their own, they are likely to be seen by themselves, by their partners, and by others as perpetrators of abuse, rather than, more accurately, as battered men defending themselves (see also Renzetti, 1992, for a description of this phenomenon among battered lesbians). Either way, a man's victimization is discounted, ignored, or mislabeled.

The police also often fail to recognize male victimization in same-sex battering. Instead, in their reports, they often label the violence they see as "mutual combat," thereby defining the victim and batterer as equally violent and accountable, and rendering the case extremely difficult to prosecute.

Services designed to help battered heterosexual women are also unlikely to be helpful to the battered gay male in acknowledging his experience of victimization. The mainstream domestic violence movement still adheres to gender-based, heterosexist theories of battering that preclude the possibility of male victims or female perpetrators of violence (Bricker, 1993; Island & Letellier, 1991). As a result, many existing domestic violence services will not provide help to *any* man, regardless of his sexual orientation or the danger he may be in. Battered gay men report that workers on domestic violence hotlines sometimes hang up on them or tell them to call batterers' treatment programs.

As a result, almost everywhere he turns, the battered male has to convince people that he has been traumatized and violated. If his perpetrator has AIDS, that task becomes even more daunting. Given the high levels of ignorance and denial about domestic violence in the gay community, it may be difficult or impossible for him to convince even his closest friends that his partner, who may look frail and weak, is abusing and terrorizing him.

Some battered gay and bisexual men report that their perpetrators with AIDS will use their diagnosis, and their sickly appearance, to manipulate the police and the criminal justice system to their advantage. For example, the batterer says, "I have AIDS. I'm too sick to hurt him . . . just look at me," and the police do not make the appropriate arrest, despite the victim's statements or injuries. Perpetrators have also tried to use this tactic to convince judges not to grant restraining orders against them.

Service providers must remember that battering is a personal choice not determined by the size, weight, physical strength, or "butchness" of any particular person. In addition to being physically abusive, men who are ill and weak can be manipulative, controlling, threatening, and otherwise psychologically abusive. The mere threat of violence is a very powerful method of control, particularly if the perpetrator has a history of physical violence against his partner (Browne, 1987). Any reference to domestic violence made by a client (for example, "We have really nasty fights," or "Sometimes things get out of hand") must be taken seriously and followed up with a series of direct questions about battering, regardless of the health status or physical appearance of the perpetrator.

Research on battered heterosexual women shows that they expect health care providers to ask questions about domestic abuse and will respond honestly to questions asked in a caring, non-judgmental manner (Council on Ethical and Judicial Affairs, 1992; Goldberg & Tomlanovich, 1984). Battered gay and bisexual men deserve the same level of care. Service providers who believe the man they are working with may be battered can say, for example, "Some of the men I work with are hurt by their male partners. Are you in a relationship with a man? Does he hurt you? Are you afraid of him?" "Many gay men are hurt by their partners. Did your boyfriend or lover hurt you?" (Letellier, 1994).

LEAVING A VIOLENT PARTNER

HIV infection can have a tremendous impact on a man's motivation and ability to leave his violent partner (Merrill, 1993). For example, both HIV-negative and HIV-positive men report that their HIV-infected partners will "play sick," faking illness in order to convince them not to leave, or to entice them back once they have left. Negative and positive men also may have lost many, or even all, of their friends to AIDS, and feel very isolated and disconnected from the community (Paul, Hayes, & Coates, forthcoming). This pervasive sense of isolation is likely to be intensified by domestic violence. Negative and positive men, like other victims of battering, also tend to blame themselves for their partner's violence and to have low self-esteem. For these men, however, internalization of the animosity in society toward gay people and people with AIDS may further contribute to their own self-denigration, thus decreasing their ability and/or willingness to escape their violent partners. The decision to leave must be made, of course, in the context of the more common difficulties associated with leaving a violent partner: lack of financial resources, lack of social support services for gay and bisexual men, and escalating violence (Browne, 1987; Island & Letellier, 1991; NiCarthy, 1986).

While the preceding examples are obstacles with which both negative and positive men must contend, these men also face a unique set of difficulties that arise as a direct result of their particular HIV status.

Difficulties in Leaving for HIV-Negative Men

There is a growing body of evidence that gay and bisexual men not infected with HIV often suffer an array of serious psychological problems as a result of the AIDS epidemic (Odets, 1990; Rosenthal, 1992; Navarro, 1993). HIV-negative men are prone to chronic anxiety, depression, sleep disorders, impaired concentration and feelings of shame, fear, hopelessness, and helplessness (Odets, 1990; Schochet, 1989). (Domestic violence experts will recognize this list as also accurately describing victims of battering.) Seronegative men also suffer what has come to be recognized as survivor guilt (Odets, 1990). These men report feeling guilty for surviving an epidemic that has taken so many of their loved ones; for not having HIV themselves; for "not doing enough" to help those afflicted with AIDS; and for being concerned about long-term goals and plans, such as pursuing higher education or opening a retirement account.

For the HIV-negative battered man, the trauma of domestic violence victimization is thus likely to be compounded by the confusing array of emotions associated with survivor guilt. Leaving his partner may mean leaving a person who may be ill or dying to fend for himself without a primary caregiver. The victim may feel he is betraying his partner and even the entire community by not staying and providing care. Leaving an HIV-infected partner who is abusive may also mean facing a circle of friends who, as part of the gay male community, do not yet consider domestic violence a serious problem.

Service providers working with HIV-negative or HIV-positive battered gay and bisexual men should follow the general feminist principles of client empowerment that characterize much of the heterosexual battered women's movement. Helpers must be able to explore the phenomenon of being HIV-negative with their clients without minimizing the psychological impact of the epidemic. Information about survivor guilt, chronic multiple loss, and grieving rituals may be useful in helping sort out clients' AIDS-related stresses from the trauma of partner violence. Access to support groups for men who are HIV-negative can also be helpful in eroding the isolation that these two epidemics create. It should also be stressed, of course, that battering is a crime and victims may have options within the criminal justice system to help protect them from their violent partners. Finally, helper providers may want to explore with their clients ways to continue to care for their partners without putting themselves in danger of more violence, such as moving out and becoming part of a team of caregivers, or never being alone with the perpetrator.

Difficulties for HIV-Positive Men

For the battered gay or bisexual man who is HIV-positive, leaving an abusive partner raises an array of concerns about caregiving, failing health, and the "taint," even in the gay male community, of being HIV-positive. More specifically, many HIV-positive battered men believe that their only hope for a satisfying, long-term relationship is to stay with their current partner, no matter how abusive he might be (Merrill, 1993). These men may feel they are "damaged goods," and view the singles dating scene as more threatening than living with a man who may be periodically violent.

For men with full-blown AIDS, leaving an abusive partner may not seem possible. Given the homophobia and AIDS-phobia in this culture, even a very sick man may be unable to turn to his family of origin for support or caregiving. In addition, many men with AIDS are on disability or other fixed incomes and may be financially dependent on their partners. In many instances, both the victim and the perpetrator have AIDS and are dependent on their joint income for survival. For these men, leaving may result in both partners losing their housing, and many battered gay men simply may be unwilling to put both themselves and their partners on the street. Like other battered people, they may prefer the familiarity of their own home, despite the danger of violence, to the unknown future beyond their front door. Especially for men who are very sick, leaving may not seem worth the effort.

Social knowledge about HIV and its related social service needs, such as housing and meals, approaches to death and loss and an understanding of gay male culture are invaluable assets for helpers working with battered gay and bisexual men who have HIV or AIDS (Ritter & O'Neill, 1989). Their ideas and feelings about their declining health, their fears about rejection, their financial limitations, and their frustrations in dealing with the social service system should be acknowledged and validated, but not seen as insurmountable barriers to a life free of abuse and violence.

CONCLUSION

HIV must be understood as a factor that complicates the lives of battered gay and bisexual men and may restrict their perceptions of alternatives to abuse, but it is not a cause of same-sex battering. Perpetrators will use HIV as yet another weapon available to them in their attempts to control their partners, a weapon with serious and possibly life-threatening implications. For gay and bisexual men, the difficulty of leaving a violent partner is exacerbated by HIV. Although they face many of the same barriers to escape that other domestic violence victims do, their sexual orientation and particular HIV status also play a role in their willingness and ability to leave.

This article highlights the desperate need for research on gay male battering. Salient questions abound: How do battered gay and bisexual men with AIDS best interact with the legal system (particularly in states with sodomy laws)? What is the relationship, if any, between HIV-related dementia and violence? How can effective relationships be forged between HIV/AIDS service providers and domestic violence service providers?

The gay and bisexual male communities around the country have been very slow to respond to the problem of same-sex battering. As a result, there is little help available to the victims of this violence. Given this context of community indifference, it is crucial for social service providers to be fluent in both the language and understanding of battering and AIDS and to help their clients unravel the paralyzing confusion created by these epidemics and explore alternatives to abuse.

REFERENCES

Barrett, D.C. (1993). *The influence of multiple identities on the health behaviors of gay men*. Unpublished doctoral dissertation, Indiana University.

Bricker, D. (1993). Fatal defense: An analysis of battered woman's syndrome expert testimony for gay men and lesbians who kill abusive partners. *Brooklyn Law Review, 58*, 1379-1437.

Browne, A. (1987). *When battered women kill*. New York: The Free Press.

Caesar, L.P., & Hamberger, L.K. (Eds.). (1989). *Treating men who batter: Theory, practice, and programs*. New York: Springer.

Centers for Disease Control (1993, February). *HIV/AIDS surveillance report*. Atlanta: U.S. Department of Health and Human Services.

Council on Ethical and Judicial Affairs, American Medical Association (1992). Physicians and domestic violence: Ethical considerations. *Journal of the American Medical Association, 267*, 3190-3193.

Farley, N. (1990, July). *Same-sex domestic violence*. Paper presented at the 12th National Lesbian and Gay Health Conference, Washington, DC.

Folkman, S., Chesney, M.A., & Christopher-Richards, A. (1993). Stress and coping in caregiving partners of men with AIDS. In L. Zegans & T.J. Coats (Eds.), *Diagnosis and management of psychiatric manifestations of HIV disease* (pp. 1-29). Philadelphia: W.B. Saunders.

Frank, P.B., & Houghton, B.O. (1987). *Confronting the batterer*. New York: Volunteer Counseling Services of Rockland County, Inc.

Goldberg, W.G., & Tomlanovich, M.C. (1984). Domestic violence victims in the emergency department: New findings. *Journal of the American Medical Association, 251*, 3259-3264.

Gondolf, E.W. (1985). *Men who batter: An integrated approach for stopping wife abuse*. Holmes Beach, FL: Learning Publications.

Harry, J., & Duvall, W.B. (1978). *The social organization of gay males*. New York: Praeger.

Island, D., & Letellier, P. (1991). *Men who beat the men who love them: Battered gay men and domestic violence*. New York: Harrington Park Press.

Jacob, S. (1993, January 24). In Hub and beyond, HIV seen as latest whip for batterers. *Boston Globe*, pp. 21, 24.

Letellier, P. (1994, April). Identifying and treating battered gay men. *San Francisco Medicine*, pp. 16-19.

Lobel, K. (Ed.). (1986). *Naming the violence: Speaking out about lesbian battering*. Seattle: Seal Press.

Merrill, G. (1993). *Positively battered: HIV and battered gay and bisexual men*. Unpublished paper.

Navarro, M. (1993, January 11). Healthy, gay, guilt-stricken: AIDS's toll on the virus-free. *New York Times*, pp. A1, A16.

NiCarthy, G. (1986). *Getting free: A handbook for women in abusive relationships*. Seattle: Seal Press.

Odets, W. (1990). The homosexualization of AIDS. *Focus: A Guide to AIDS Research and Counseling, 5,* 1-2.

Paul, J.P., Hayes, R.B., & Coates, T.J. (forthcoming). The impact of the HIV epidemic on U.S. gay male communities. In A.R. D'Augelli & C.J. Patterson (Eds.), *Lesbian, gay, and bisexual identities over the lifespan: Psychological perspectives on personal, relational and community processes.* London: Oxford University Press.

Peterson, J.L., & Marin, G. (1988). Issues in the prevention of AIDS among black and Hispanic men. *American Psychologist, 43,* 871-877.

Renzetti, C. (1992). *Violent betrayal: Partner abuse in lesbian relationships.* Newbury Park, CA: Sage Publications.

Ritter, K.Y., & O'Neill, C.W. (1989). Moving through the loss: The spiritual journey of gay men and lesbian women. *Journal of Counseling and Development, 68,* 9-15.

Rosenthal, E. (1992, December 6). Struggling to handle bereavement as AIDS rips relationships apart. *New York Times,* pp. A1, A21.

Russell, D.E.H. (1982). *Rape in marriage.* New York: Macmillan.

San Francisco Department of Public Health AIDS Office (1994, July 31). *AIDS surveillance report.*

San Francisco Sentinel (1994, August 10). San Francisco gay men ignoring safe sex, p. 7.

Schochet, R. (1989). Psychosocial issues for seronegative gay men in San Francisco. *Focus: A Guide to AIDS Research and Counseling, 4,* 3.

Schulman, D. (1991). AIDS discrimination: Its nature, meaning, and function. In N. McKenzie (Ed.), *The AIDS reader: Social, political, and ethical issues* (pp. 463-490). New York: Meridian Books.

Sinclair, H. (1990, May). *Not her, him.* Paper presented to the San Francisco District Attorney's Office and General Works, San Francisco, CA.

Sonkin, D.J., & Durphy, M. (1989). *Learning to live without violence.* Volcano, CA: Volcano Press.

Szymanski, M. (1991, Fall). Battered husbands: Domestic violence in gay relationships. *Genre,* pp. 32, 73.

Tuller, D. (1994, January 3). When gays batter their partners. *San Francisco Chronicle,* pp. 1, 8.

Walker, L.E. (1979). *The battered woman.* New York: Harper & Row.

Intervention in Gay Male
Intimate Violence Requires
Coordinated Efforts on Multiple Levels

L. Kevin Hamberger

SUMMARY. Research and understanding of partner violence among gay male couples are currently in rudimentary form. Gay male domestic violence must be analyzed and understood at multiple levels. A sociopolitical analysis includes naming the problem while coordinating efforts with domestic violence programs in the heterosexual community. Specific remedies include developing safe-house networks, educating mental health professionals and working for legislative remedies. Individual-level analyses and interventions include assessment of personality and psychopathology, problem-solving deficits, and function and pattern of violence. Interventions focus on behavior change in the batterer. Recommendations for research based on these multiple levels of analysis and intervention are discussed. *[Article copies available from The Haworth Document Delivery Service: 1-800-342-9678.]*

L. Kevin Hamberger, PhD, is a clinical psychologist and Professor of Clinical Family and Community Medicine in the Department of Family and Community Medicine, Medical College of Wisconsin. For the past ten years, he has conducted a program of treatment and research with domestically violent men. He is the Chair of the Group on Violence Education for the Society of Teachers of Family Medicine, and serves on the Wisconsin Governor's Council on Domestic Abuse.

Correspondence may be addressed to the author at St. Catherine's Family Practice Center, Medical College of Wisconsin, Tallent Hall, P.O. Box 598, Kenosha, WI 53141.

[Haworth co-indexing entry note]: "Intervention in Gay Male Intimate Violence Requires Coordinated Efforts on Multiple Levels." Hamberger, L. Kevin. Co-published simultaneously in *Journal of Gay & Lesbian Social Services* (The Haworth Press, Inc.) Vol. 4, No. 1, 1996, pp. 83-91; and: *Violence in Gay and Lesbian Domestic Partnerships* (ed: Claire M. Renzetti, and Charles Harvey Miley), The Haworth Press, Inc., 1996, pp. 83-91; and: *Violence in Gay and Lesbian Domestic Partnerships* (ed: Claire M. Renzetti, and Charles Harvey Miley) Harrington Park Press, an imprint of The Haworth Press, Inc., 1996, pp. 83-91. Single or multiple copies of this article are available from The Haworth Document Delivery Service [1-800-342-9678, 9:00 a.m. - 5:00 p.m. (EST)].

INTRODUCTION

Over the past fifteen years, activists and social scientists interested in domestic violence have focused almost exclusively on male-to-female violence in heterosexual relationships. Little is known about the incidence and prevalence of gay partner assault. Current estimates suggesting high rates of violence in gay intimate relationships are based on small, highly selected samples or extrapolations from epidemiological surveys of heterosexuals. Forty-seven percent of gay men reported violence in their relationships in one study (Kelly & Warshafsky, 1987), but the sample size was small. On the other hand, Island and Letellier (1991a) estimated that 350,000 to 650,000 gay males are battered by their intimate partners each year, approximately the same rate of battering found in heterosexual couples.

Intimate relationship violence is sufficiently widespread in both heterosexual and gay male relationships to constitute a public health problem (Koop, 1987), justifying sociopolitical analysis. However, there is a strong need for research with gay male populations, as we cannot generalize findings about intimate partner violence from one subgroup to another. For example, while gender issues are important in heterosexual intimate violence, they may be less relevant, or take a substantially different form, in homosexual relationships (Island, 1992; Letellier, 1992). Any research or analysis must concede the possibility that "the problem" is really "the problems," including modifications to fit the experience of diverse groups.

This paper focuses on the integration of social and community-level interventions with direct, individual-level services to confront gay male partner batterers and provide safety to victims. The integrated approach challenges the entire community, gay and straight alike, to acknowledge and work together to eradicate violent behaviors. Some of the information may also apply to lesbian batterers–another understudied group–but the reader should be as cautious about extrapolating information from one homosexual group to another as from heterosexual to homosexual populations.

INDIVIDUAL ANALYSIS AND INTERVENTION

Although the problem of gay and other intimate partner violence is a broad social issue requiring major reform, direct intervention is the first and most immediate concern in any given instance of battering (Hamberger & Lohr, 1989; Letellier, 1992). Direct intervention is required for the safety of the victim, and for the perpetrator to learn alternative, nonviolent behaviors. Therefore, while societal-level interventions constitute an overarching approach to stopping violence, individual or psychological processes must be considered when conducting direct interventions.

Batterer Characteristics

Heterosexual male batterers have been shown to be a heterogeneous population encompassing a number of personality disorders (Hamberger & Hastings, 1988). Moreover, batterers are more likely than nonbatterers to attribute negative intent to hypothetical behaviors of their heterosexual partners (Holtzworth-Munroe, 1992); they are also less assertive and more hostile (Maiuro, Cahn, & Vitaliano, 1986; Maiuro, Cahn, Vitaliano, Wagner, & Zegree, 1988). There are no reports in the literature of characteristics of perpetrators of gay male partner violence, but Island and Letellier (1991) hypothesize that gay male batterers exhibit similar psychological characteristics to their heterosexual counterparts. However, research must include gay batterer samples if we wish to move beyond speculation.

Psychological Analysis

Individual, behavioral, and psychological analyses set the stage for optimal interventions. These analyses shed light on the proximal causes of violence, illuminating intervention targets. In a clinical setting, such assessment includes a detailed clinical history. Assessment of violence parameters, including history, duration, course (getting more or less severe), and frequency should also be conducted. Assessment also includes exploring, with the offender, the meaning and function of his violence. Various beliefs related to violence, conflict, and relationship roles should be examined, as well as skills in nonviolent coping. Personality and other psychological assessments can provide clues about specific personality disorders or problem-solving deficits, as well as substance abuse or psychiatric problems.

Some activists fear that psychological analysis will relieve the batterer of responsibility for his actions, blaming instead his personality disorder or other problems. Hamberger and Hastings (1988), however, have argued that elucidation of personality disorders and other factors provides useful information regarding:

1. selection of treatment targets;
2. prognosis and length of therapy; and
3. risk of dropping out of treatment or of recidivism.

Island and Letellier (1991a) emphasize the importance of placing responsibility for violence on the perpetrator, rather than on society. An analysis which so directs personal responsibility also focuses attention on the intrapersonal functions of violence, which include punishment, domination, and control.

THE NEED FOR MULTIPLE-LEVEL INTERVENTION EFFORTS

Individual analysis will impact a few dozen couples each year, but it will have no effect on the widespread problem of partner abuse. For change to take place, the social forces which effectively condone or sustain intimate partner violence must be altered. Indeed, U.S. society has a high tolerance for all forms of violence. Gays, in particular, are a group which, in addition to being generally oppressed, are targeted for violence that often has little or no legal or social consequences. Thus, in conceptualizing interventions, one must conceptualize changes in the fabric of social values and practices that support violence toward vulnerable populations. To be effective, individual interventions must take place in the context of societal and community interventions. In this network, the act of conducting therapy communicates a consistent social message that intimate partner violence is wrong and will not be condoned.

Among the social factors impeding both analysis of the problem and intervention are collective denial of intimate partner violence in general and heterosexism and oppression of homosexuals. The gay male community itself often denies partner violence (Island & Letellier, 1991a).

An integrated approach to gay male batterer interventions includes educating members of the gay community and others, working within the criminal justice system, developing safe-house networks for victims, and ensuring the quality of treatment programs.

COMMUNITY AND SOCIETAL LEVEL INTERVENTIONS

Naming the Problem

Naming the problem is the first step in motivating community leaders to recognize the problem and confront denial. Thus, general community education about the incidence and prevalence of such violence is a necessary basic intervention in both homosexual and heterosexual communities. In one model education intervention, the New York City Gay and Lesbian Anti-Violence Project distributed 5,000 posters with a help hotline telephone number in New York City subway cars (Island & Letellier, 1991b).

Establishing Community Networks

If education about gay male battering is to be effective, an organized, coordinated, community network must be in place to provide avenues for studying, advocating change, and educating the community about partner violence. Examples of existing coordinated projects include the Domestic Violence Program of the Gay and Lesbian Community Action Council of St. Paul, Minnesota, and the National Lesbian and Gay Health Association, Washington, D.C.

Batterer and victim programs should work to develop and participate in community and state task forces on partner abuse. Such task forces would include judges, police, prosecutors, victim advocates, batterer therapists, social service personnel, clergy, medical professionals, and community leaders. Working together, representatives of these community sectors can effect change in ways that individuals and isolated programs cannot. This joint approach also lifts the burden of finding solutions from any one segment and distributes it among the entire community, where responsibility should be lodged.

One of the solutions, and another shared community task, is the development of safe-house networks for victims. Special concerns of homosexual intimate violence victims, such as fear of being identified or discriminated against in programs designed for heterosexuals, must be addressed and remedied at the community and programmatic levels, as part of a cooperative, unified effort.

Research and Program Development in the Criminal Justice System

On the local community level, gay domestic violence experts can work for change in policies and procedures for intervening with perpetrators and victims. The first step is conducting surveys to ascertain the incidence of gay male domestic violence. Surveys can assess victims' experiences with police, the courts, and other protective and social service agencies. Also useful is a court-watch program to monitor prosecution and sentencing patterns in cases of gay male domestic violence. Empowered by data from this research, advocates for victims can develop training programs enabling police and other members of the judicial system to recognize and respond appropriately to the seriousness of gay male partner violence (Letellier, 1992). Another key task is to ensure appropriate treatment referrals and communicate information about client compliance and participation to the referral source.

Educating Mental Health Professionals

Mental health professionals also benefit from education about gay male partner violence (Hansen & Harway, 1992). Although these professionals may not perform actual interventions, they may be the first point of contact for gay perpetrators and victims. Enhanced knowledge of service networks can facilitate identification, assessment, and appropriate referrals in cases of gay domestic violence. Individual therapists may also wish to develop additional expertise and incorporate gay male batterers or victims or both into their clientele.

Coordinating Efforts with the Heterosexual Community

Experts on gay domestic violence can educate experts in heterosexual partner violence and, where possible, integrate efforts. For example, members of the gay community can work with those who have established shelters and safe-house networks for heterosexual women and children. By combining respective expertise, such a task force can develop a network of safe houses for gay male victims. Such combining of forces and activities communicates a united voice confronting all forms of violence in intimate relationships. Similarly, therapists of gay male offenders who focus on long-term personality-based approaches (e.g., Farley, 1992) can share their knowledge and expertise with therapists of heterosexual groups which tend to focus primarily on short-term, behavior modification approaches. Therapists who see individual clients might receive further training in the issues of gay domestic violence.

Legislative Interventions

As gay victims of partner violence have not been afforded equal treatment under the law, social analysis and interventions aimed at impacting policy and legislative change are crucial. Some legislative reforms are being attempted, such as efforts to modify California statutes to include homosexual relationships in domestic violence arrest laws (Island & Letellier, 1991c). Concerted lobbying efforts by united groups of community advocates are more likely to be effective than individual actions.

CONCLUSION

Violence between intimate partners is a social epidemic, although we continue to deny the proportions of the epidemic. The problem is probably as large among gay males as it is among heterosexual couples; however, little research has been done to determine the incidence and delineate specific characteristics of partner abuse in gay couples, and the gay community tends to deny the problem of partner violence just as the heterosexual community does. Much of what is known about heterosexual partner violence may be generalizable to gay male partners or others, but we must be cautious in making such assumptions.

Individual interventions are the first step in protecting and offering help to the victim and attempting to change the behavior of the batterer. However, individual interventions must take place in the context of broader community and societal-level interventions. These include research, education across the board, program development and reform in the criminal justice system, batterer intervention programs including safe-house networks, and legislative reform. Key participants in effecting change are judges, police, prosecutors, victim advocates, batterer and victim therapists, social service professionals, clergy, physicians, and community leaders.

A coordinated effort uses the rich resources of the entire community to solve problems. It also acknowledges that the problem is one affecting society, and not an isolated aberration. While the perpetrator must be held accountable for his actions at every step through the intervention process, the community at large must be held accountable for ensuring the safety of victims and assigning responsibility to batterers. The community also is responsible for raising a unified voice protesting all forms of violence, including that against intimate partners.

REFERENCES

Farley, N. (1992, October). Working with gay abusers: Parts I and II, theory and practice. Workshop presented at the conference on Double Jeopardy: Confronting Same-Sex Domestic Violence, St. Paul, MN.

Hamberger, L.K., & Hastings, J.E. (1988). Characteristics of male spouse abusers consistent with personality disorders. *Hospital and Community Psychiatry, 39,* 763-770.

Hamberger, L.K., & Lohr, J.M. (1989). Proximal causes of spouse abuse: Cognitive and behavioral factors. In P.L. Caesar & L.K. Hamberger (Eds.), *Treating men who batter: Theory, practice, and programs* (pp. 53-76). New York: Springer.

Hansen, M., & Harway, M. (1992, August). Psychologists as consultants on family violence. Paper presented at the Annual Meeting of the American Psychological Association, Washington, DC.

Holtzworth-Munroe, A. (1992). Attributions and maritally violent men: The role of cognitions in marital violence. In J. Harvey, T.L. Orbuch, & A.L. Weber (Eds.), *Attributions, accounts, and close relationships* (pp. 165-175). New York: Springer-Verlag.

Island, D. (1992, August). *Battering disorders: Individual causation theory alternatives to heterosexist sociopolitical theory.* Paper presented at the Annual Meeting of the American Psychological Association. Washington, DC.

Island, D., & Letellier, P. (1991a). *Men who beat the men who love them.* New York: Harrington Park Press.

Island, D., & Letellier, P. (1991b, Fall). 5,000 posters on gay lesbian domestic violence placed on NYC subways. *Gay and Lesbian Domestic Violence Network Newsletter,* pp. 1-2.

Island, D., & Letellier, P. (1991c, Fall). Heterosexist domestic violence laws deny many gays and lesbians full civil rights. *Gay and Lesbian Domestic Violence Network Newsletter,* p. 3.

Kelly, C.E., & Warshafsky, L. (1987, July). *Partner abuse in gay male and lesbian relationships.* Paper presented at the Third National Family Violence Research Conference, Durham, NH.

Koop, C.E. (1987, September). *Healing interpersonal violence: Making health a full partner.* Keynote address at the Surgeon General's Northwest Conference on Interpersonal Violence, Seattle, WA.

Letellier, P. (1992, August). *Gay male victimization in domestic violence: How non-female experiences challenge current theory.* Paper presented at the Annual Meeting of the American Psychological Association, Washington, DC.

Maiuro, R.D., Cahn, T.S., & Vitaliano, P.P. (1986). Assertiveness and hostility in domestically violent men. *Violence and Victims, 1,* 279-289.

Maiuro, E.D., Cahn, T.S., Vitaliano, P.P., Wagner, B.C., & Zegree, J.B. (1988). Anger, hostility, and depression in domestically violent versus generally assaultive men and nonviolent control subjects. *Journal of Consulting and Clinical Psychology, 56,* 17-23.

Couple Assessment: Identifying and Intervening in Domestic Violence in Lesbian Relationships

Arlene Istar

SUMMARY. This paper examines the three paradigms that intersect when working with lesbian couples affected by domestic violence. The intersection of these three paradigms–family systems theory, lesbian and gay affirmative therapy, and the feminist analysis of domestic violence–creates a dilemma for lesbian therapists working in rural areas or small cities. Without the support of domestic violence services developed for or within the lesbian community, or a lesbian/gay community committed to acknowledging domestic violence, the lesbian affirmative therapist must balance the needs of the lesbian client with the feminist analysis of violence. This article outlines strategies that protect abused lesbians, without prematurely sacrificing the lesbian couple's relationship. *[Article copies available from The Haworth Document Delivery Service: 1-800-342-9678.]*

Arlene S. Istar, CSW, CAC, is a founding member of Choices Counseling Associates, a therapy collective committed to affirmative counseling services for lesbian, gay, bisexual, and transgendered people. Choices is located outside of Albany, NY. Ms. Istar is also an adjunct faculty member at the Graduate School of Social Welfare, S.U.N.Y., Albany.

Correspondence may be addressed to the author at 266 Delaware Avenue, Delmar, NY 12054.

[Haworth co-indexing entry note]: "Couple Assessment: Identifying and Intervening in Domestic Violence in Lesbian Relationships." Istar, Arlene. Co-published simultaneously in *Journal of Gay & Lesbian Social Services* (The Haworth Press, Inc.) Vol. 4, No. 1, 1996, pp. 93-106; and: *Violence in Gay and Lesbian Domestic Partnerships* (ed: Claire M. Renzetti, and Charles Harvey Miley), The Haworth Press, Inc., 1996, pp. 93-106; and: *Violence in Gay and Lesbian Domestic Partnerships* (ed: Claire M. Renzetti, and Charles Harvey Miley) Harrington Park Press, an imprint of The Haworth Press, Inc., 1996, pp. 93-106. Single or multiple copies of this article are available from The Haworth Document Delivery Service [1-800-342-9678, 9:00 a.m. - 5:00 p.m. (EST)].

93

Domestic violence in lesbian partnerships has become an issue of increasing public awareness in both the domestic violence movement and the gay and lesbian press in recent years. The focus of research and political activism has been to bring attention to the high incidence of abuse in lesbian and gay relationships. However, there has been a dearth of information on how to clinically address the needs of gays and lesbians who are involved in relationships that are actively violent and abusive.

This paper represents a beginning attempt to develop clinical assessment tools to recognize abusive dynamics and strategies and to interrupt them. It is especially important that as therapists we examine our assessment and intervention tools since, as Claire Renzetti (1992) has pointed out from her research on lesbian battering, over half of her participants sought help from a counselor. Although the focus of this paper is on lesbian couples, I believe that many of the ideas I am presenting will be applicable to gay male relationships and perhaps heterosexual relationships as well. It is also important to bear in mind that some women in lesbian relationships are bisexually identified, which can be a source of conflict between women.

THREE TREATMENT PARADIGMS

Treating lesbian and gay domestic violence demands the alliance of at least three different theoretical paradigms. The first is the feminist sociopolitical analysis of patriarchal violence, which is the foundation of the domestic violence movement.

The current movement against lesbian battering has been built on the experiences of the (heterosexual) battered women's movement, and interventions have been geared towards assisting lesbians who are currently being battered to leave abusive relationships. An effective political campaign created by lesbians within the domestic violence movement has addressed homophobia in the shelters through community education (Geraci, 1986; Porat, 1986). Consequently, in some larger cities, lesbians seeking shelter from violence have not only been believed, but have been able to receive sufficient community support in the form of concrete services. Services for gay male victims are being developed following a similar model of ending abusive relationships and receiving support usually through group work (Island & Letellier, 1991). Despite the raised consciousness of the domestic violence community regarding the needs of lesbians and gay men, shelters, especially in smaller cities, are already functioning on less than adequate financial resources and, consequently, are often unable to incorporate the special needs of battered lesbians (or men, homosexual or heterosexual) into their already overburdened system.

Batterers programs have been receiving increased attention in the domestic violence literature, often at the expense of services for victims (Davis, 1987). Questions, however, remain about the efficacy of batterers services. Rarely, if ever, are these services geared towards, or appropriate for, lesbian batterers.

This current treatment milieu is predicated on the separation of victim from perpetrator. This system was developed with the primary aims of protecting and empowering the battered woman. As long as the battered woman is under the control of her batterer, she is not able to speak freely about her experience and, furthermore, is in potential danger that afterwards the batterer will further victimize her for the information she shared in front of a third party. Family therapist Daniel Willback (1989) has said that "when a potentially actively violent abuser and the abused person are in the same family, family therapy may be generally contraindicated" (p. 50). Barbara Pressman (1989), also a family therapist, echoes this, agreeing that "the primary consideration in working with abused women is their safety" (p. 32).

The second paradigm that interfaces here is the development of lesbian and gay affirmative therapy. This approach assumes that homosexuality and homosexual relationships are normal and healthy lifestyles. Lesbian and gay affirmative therapy has developed in direct reaction to a homophobic social service system that has ignored, trivialized and, at its worst, blatantly mistreated lesbians and gay men. At its best, the social service system still remains ignorant of the life issues facing lesbian, gay and bisexual people. (For discussions of lesbian and gay affirmative therapy, see Boston Lesbian Psychologies Collective, 1987; Gonsiorek, 1985; Silverstein, 1991).

The third paradigm, family systems therapy, has also been essential to the development of lesbian and gay affirmative counseling. In order to effectively work with lesbian couples, a therapist must recognize the various systems that are interconnected, including the family of origin, the family of choice, the extended friendship network, and the lesbian community context that has birthed and nurtured an environment in which lesbian couples can create families. (This is not to deny the historical and cross-cultural existence of lesbians and lesbian families, or to ignore lesbians who are only minimally connected to the lesbian community. However, the role of the feminist, and gay and lesbian civil rights movements in identity development for lesbians, and lesbian families, cannot be overemphasized.) As part of affirming lesbian identity, it is appropriate to acknowledge couple commitments and the bonds of families of choice that are not recognized legally, and often not honored socially. Lesbian family therapy insists that we treat lesbians within the context of their families and communities.

A number of difficulties are immediately apparent at the intersection of these three paradigms.

First, the intervention strategies borrowed from the feminist domestic violence movement assume the existence of a politically active lesbian and gay community committed to ending abuse and the support of a domestic violence community committed to ending homophobia. Outside of large cities, there are few alternatives to the homophobic service system, and rarely are there specialized domestic violence services that are sensitive to lesbian and gay issues. Therapists working with lesbians and gay men in small cities and rural areas need effective assessment and intervention techniques that do not assume the availability of shelters, services for batterers, and safe home networks. Even the development of empowerment groups requires a certain number of willing participants. Although in large cities these conditions typically exist, the majority of battered lesbians and gay men do not have access to these supportive services.

The second difficulty that arises is the dual role of a lesbian affirmative therapist. Working within a homophobic system, lesbian affirmative therapists must be aware of the possibility that other agencies are minimizing the impact of domestic violence between women, and/or are minimizing the functional potential of lesbian partnerships. The lesbian affirmative therapist working with battered lesbians is often placed in the conflicting role of supporting lesbian families in an often hostile and homophobic environment on one hand, and intervening in dysfunctional, abusive, and fused relationships on the other.

In one case, for example, I had spent many months in an inpatient addiction agency developing a gay affirmative program and training the staff to respect lesbian families. A lesbian was completing the program and returning to the rural farm where she lived with her violently abusive lover. Although she had arrived in treatment with bruises and expressed terror about the prospect of returning home, her case manager was unable to honestly examine the violence because he wanted to appear supportive of the lesbian relationship.

Lesbians entering therapy are desperate to have their relationships recognized as legitimate. To attempt to prematurely sever that couple bond by suggesting separate treatment, especially when that treatment does not even exist, can instead prematurely sever the therapeutic bond, leaving the violent relationship intact.

In another case, a lesbian couple presented with obvious signs of battering. As soon as I was able to detect any sign of violence, I immediately recommended separate treatment. The batterer became so jealous and enraged about what she imagined her lover was saying in individual therapy that she abruptly ended therapy, deciding instead that "they" would do couple counseling with a heterosexual male psychiatrist.

However well-intentioned the clinical resistance to "couple counseling," an issue I will address next, sometimes battered women request conjoint services and to refuse, no matter how clinically or politically correct, means the client will probably go elsewhere, and elsewhere will often mean a therapist ignorant of battering issues.

The third difficulty, and by far the most complicated, has been the sexist denial of violence and power and control dynamics that has been endemic in the family systems field. Although this issue deserves far more attention than I have the space for in this article, many feminist family therapists have been addressing these issues for the past 10 years (Bagarozzi & Giddings, 1983; Bograd, 1984;

Goldner, 1992; Goldner, Penn, Sheinberg, & Walker, 1990; Margolin, 1982; Margolin, Fernandez, Talovic, & Onorato, 1983; Willback, 1989). In the past, family therapists have viewed both partners as participants in the violence which served a homeostatic function. MacKinnon and Miller (1987) criticize this "notion of reciprocity . . . [which] . . . implies that participants are not only mutually, but *equally,* involved in maintaining the interaction . . . , creating a reality in which all family members appear to be equally responsible" (p. 144, author's emphasis). This argument against mutual responsibility has resounded throughout the feminist domestic violence literature. For example:

> Feminism challenges most family therapists' idea that in a circular world people are reciprocally powerful and helpless, with no one carrying more weight than another. It raises the question of whether a therapist can really be neutral about power. (Bepko, 1985, p. 47)

This lack of understanding of the dynamics of domestic violence among family therapists, and their disrespect for the actual danger battered women face, has fractionalized domestic violence treatment, making even the suggestion of "couple counseling" anathema. Couple therapy is deemed far too dangerous for battered women. For instance, Schechter (1987) states:

> Couples therapy is an inappropriate intervention that further endangers the woman. It encourages the abuser to blame the victim by examining her "role" in his problem. By seeing the couple, the therapist erroneously suggests that the partner, too, is responsible for the abuser's behavior. Many women have been beaten brutally following couple counseling sessions in which they disclosed violence or coercion. The abuser alone must take responsibility for the assaults. (p. 16)

Although this position was initially held by feminists working in the domestic violence movement in opposition to family therapists, many feminist family therapists are now developing systemic strategies that do not blame the victim for her abuse and do hold the abuser completely accountable for his behavior. According to Goldner (1992):

. . . both traditions have been deeply compromised by their oppositional relationship to one another. Ideas that could inform and transform one another, creating a morally and psychically complex paradigm, have instead been set against one another, creating unworkable choices between politically correct dogmas and morally timid evasions. (p. 60)

This polarization has also taken place in the lesbian battering movement. The lesbian domestic violence movement has always denounced the idea of "mutual battering" because it has been determined that one partner always wields considerably more power and control and, when battered women are violent, it is their attempt at self-defense (Hammond, 1986; Renzetti, 1992). The inherent power imbalance between abuser and victim changes the meaning of a violent act. Consequently, the proscription against "couple counseling" has been maintained in the lesbian and gay domestic violence movement.

ASSESSMENT

As a lesbian, and a feminist family therapist specializing in domestic violence, I have often felt myself torn by these opposing paradigms. I know it is inappropriate and dangerous to work with a battered woman with her batterer present, but I also know that lesbians have strong familial bonds to one another that they have created within a hostile and homophobic culture. Prematurely suggesting separation often tightens their protection of the relationship.

It is, of course, always my primary goal in working with battered women to ensure their safety. I have discovered over time, however, that insisting on separating battered women from their partners is not always the best way to ensure their safety. As Jay Haley and Chloe Madanes (1992) have noted, the couple does live together and whatever treatment modality I choose, most of their relationship takes place outside of my office. Pressman (1989) has suggested the following guidelines for couple treatment:

When a man [sic] has taken responsibility for his violent behavior; when a woman has a restored sense of her own worth and believes in her right to assert her views; when the violence has ended; when a woman no longer fears her partner; and when both the husband and wife agree to couple counselling, then couple work can begin. (p. 33)

I agree with these guidelines, but I would add to them that couples can, and indeed should, be seen together for the purposes of assessment. As Bagarozzi and Giddings (1983) propose, it may be necessary to utilize couple counseling to "gain entrance into the couple system, to overcome initial resistances and to keep the violent spouse from prematurely terminating" (p. 10).

In the domestic violence movement, the concern legitimately has been protecting abused women. When the reality that women were beating and raping other women began to get some attention in the lesbian and gay media, there was a shocked silence, followed by an outcry that it was not true. As much as we may want to deny that lesbian battering exists in lesbian relationships, or in our communities, and as righteously angry as we may be at batterers, we, as feminists, cannot dismiss woman batterers as easily as we did male batterers. As Madanes (1990, p. xiv) says, "In a family there is always the victim and the victimizer, the good and the evil, the joyful and the pathetic. The therapist is an accomplice to all and loyal to all." This, too, is true for the lesbian family. Of course, there are times when our advocacy for a battered partner must take "precedence over the goals of the family as a system" (Margolin, 1982, p. 790). However, we also must accept our loyalty to the humanity of the abusive partner. Both lives are of value. It is one thing for a survivor to insist that her batterer is "incurable"–understandable, and perhaps essential to her healing; it is quite another thing for therapists to bring this assumption into the treatment milieu.

The assessment process is essential because it is rare for a lesbian, or a lesbian couple, to come into therapy requesting treatment for domestic violence. Women often present wanting treatment for "relationship problems" or difficulties with depression, anxiety, or substance abuse. It becomes the therapist's job to determine if domestic violence is a problem. Even when women are able to name violence as a problem, this does not mean that they see it through the same political or clinical screen that the therapist does.

In heterosexual domestic violence, due to the nature of sexism and male dominance, it is easy to identify the power and control issues along gender lines, i.e., men have the power to control and women are victimized by their physically, economically, and sexually lower social position. In lesbian partnerships it is more difficult to determine the power roles, since they are not ascribed according to gender (Hammond, 1989; Renzetti, 1992). Hammond (1989) points out:

> When a lesbian requests services, there is no simple way to know that she is, indeed, the victim. In fact, because of the detrimental effects of emotional abuse, the battered lesbian often perceives herself as the one in the wrong, the one who has provoked or caused the abuse by her misbehavior. Lesbian batterers have been known to contact shelters seeking a place to stay, and identify themselves as victims. In cases in which there has been mutual verbal or physical abuse, shelter or advocacy staff may feel ill-prepared to assess which partner is "most eligible" for services. (p. 96)

The assumption is often that the batterers are identifying as victims in order to manipulate both the battered woman and the shelter staff. It is my belief that the batterer actually does *feel* victimized in many cases. It is only by understanding her perception that we can assist her in seeing the reality of her behavior.

Many lesbian couples who are able to recognize the violence in their relationship *as* violence define this violence as mutual battering. It is easy to see how this could be psychologically easier to accept than the reality of victimization, and it is also easy to imagine that the batterer would be invested in maintaining this illusion.

In communities where lesbian battering is being discussed, accusations of domestic violence can be used to scapegoat women, or as excuses to end dissatisfactory relationships. In one case, for instance, a lesbian who is a domestic violence shelter worker accused her lover of abusive behavior. When we explored this in therapy she was, in reality, ashamed that her own behavior might be abusive. The words battering and abuse, like the word addiction, can be overused, and become weapons that we hurl at each other whenever we do not like someone's behavior.

It is not always so complicated–sometimes one partner is clearly physically or psychologically abusive towards her lover, and the other partner is clearly frightened and protective. This is visible in watching body language and listening for verbal responses. Some useful questions to think about are: Does one woman always defer to the other? Does she change her opinion, or change the subject, after witnessing her partner's response? Are there bruises? Is one partner in control of the money, the car, or the children? Do they avoid eye contact or sit too close together? The therapist will need to be attuned to different signals depending on the stage of the violent cycle in which the couple currently is, and the severity of the violence (Douglas, 1991; Taylor, 1984).

As a therapist in private practice, I am ultimately left with the woman, or the couple, sitting in my office describing the dynamics of their relationship from their own perspective. They rarely talk about power and control issues, or use words like violence and abuse, and certainly do not fit into my neatly defined political definitions. My work ultimately demands that I go back to rule number one of social work: start where the client is. For example, Marie first came to see me because her lover, Pam, had asked her to go into counseling to address her frequent angry outbursts. Marie was clearly volatile and opinionated; she described furious fits of yelling, cursing, and throwing things and was ashamed that her lover was afraid of her. Marie was able to examine her behavior with insight, including her marijuana abuse, but the more she was able to control her own abusive behavior, the more depressed she became. When I invited Pam in for a couple session, she arrived in my office loud and furious. She walked up to me, her face inches from mine, her index finger poking me in the chest demanding that I "fix" Marie, and insisting that everything in the relationship was Marie's fault, and that if I couldn't fix Marie, then she would. Pam was unable to take any responsibility for any of the dynamics of the relationship, nor was she able to allow me to complete a sentence. She yelled and screamed loudly, giving me a detailed outline of Marie's "treatment plan," and finally, in frustration, walked out of my office, slamming the door behind her. Marie remained curled in a ball on my couch, rocking in silence.

When I asked Marie to invite Pam into counseling, I knew I was breaking the sacred rule of domestic violence work by potentially exposing Pam to increased violence, but I somehow felt that I was not seeing a full picture. It is clear that although Marie's behavior was often violent, much of this was in reaction to living with a woman who was extremely abusive and who was degrading her. Marie often reacted to Pam's controlling behavior with angry outbursts. It took Marie many months of therapy to even acknowledge that there was anything unacceptable about Pam's behavior; for eight years she had been manipulated into seeing Pam's violence as her fault. Without an opportunity to meet Pam and assess their dynamics as a couple, the reality of the power and control issues never would have emerged.

Another case also illustrates this point. When Sue first came into my office, she was furious at her lover, Jane, for refusing to make love to her. It was not difficult to identify Sue's behavior as classically abusive; she admitted to physical, verbal, and sexual violence readily, without any remorse or embarrassment. She saw these as appropriate ways to treat her partner. Jane was not allowed to leave the house without permission, and certainly would not be allowed to see me without Sue being present. Even this took many months to arrange. She was a surprisingly articulate woman, who was easily able to describe her situation and was not at all surprised to hear it defined as abusive. In my presence, Sue was quiet and respectful, and for the first time began to exhibit remorse. When I shared my concern with Jane that working with the two of them together might endanger her further, she laughed. "I live in potential danger all the time," she said. "I love her and I'm not leaving. If your presence can keep her this mellow, then I'm coming back, whether she likes it or not!" In front of Sue I was able to give Jane resources for a local shelter, set up guidelines for safety, and tell Sue some potential legal and criminal consequences for her violence. After a few "couple sessions," I was able to convince both partners to work individually with me, and to continue to work occasionally as a couple.

In this example, again breaking all the rules of domestic violence counseling, my presence was able to serve as a "conscience" or "superego" for Sue. Somehow she was unable to treat Jane abusively in front of me; I became the witness for her to see truly her own behavior. She later said that as she began to act in abusive ways, she could feel my presence in the room, and would decide to take a walk or call a friend instead of acting violently.

CONCLUSION

Therapists are not protecting lesbians who are battered by hiding behind the cloak of a politically correct paradigm and ignoring the client's own experience of her problems. While the safety of the battered partner is always of primary importance, in order to accurately diagnose the nature of power and control dynamics within the relationship, it may be necessary to work with both partners initially in an assessment process. An effective treatment model must address not just the limitations and dangers of "couple counseling," but also honor the systemic issues the couple brings to therapy. In respecting the clients' perceptions of their relationship, the therapist can assist them in reframing the issues. The therapist must be able to identify and assess the violence in the relationship and then assist the couple in redefining the "relationship problem."

In order to develop appropriate individual treatment plans, clinicians need to ensure that the clients are presenting accurate information. Witnessing the partners' interactions will enable the therapist to have the clearest picture of the relationship. Assessing battering in lesbian couples is a delicate process with the goals of both ensuring the protection of the battered lesbian and creating an environment where both women feel respected enough to be willing to enter into a therapeutic relationship outside of couple counseling. A thorough and careful assessment that respects the lesbian couple's relationship becomes the intervention that enables treatment to take place. The goal of therapy becomes helping lesbians build healthy partnerships, which in many cases might mean ending the relationship, but in some cases may mean developing a violence-free relationship. In the absence of supportive services, the dynamic relationship between the client(s) and the therapist is *the* treatment milieu.

REFERENCES

Bagarozzi, D.A., & Giddings, C.W. (1983). Conjugal violence: A critical review of current research and clinical practices. *American Journal of Family Therapy, 11*, 3-15.

Bepko, C. (1985, November/December). Power, power, who's got the power? *Family Therapy Networker*, pp. 47-49.

Bograd, M. (1984). Family systems approaches to wife battering: A feminist critique. *American Journal of Orthopsychiatry, 54*, 558-568.

Boston Lesbian Psychologies Collective (Eds.). (1987). *Lesbian psychologies: Explorations and challenges*. Urbana: University of Illinois Press.

Davis, L.V. (1987). Battered women: The transformation of a social problem. *Social Work, 32*, 306-311.

Douglas, H. (1991). Assessing violent couples. *Families in Society: Journal of Contemporary Human Services, 16*, 525-533.

Geraci, L. (1986). Making shelters safe for lesbians. In K. Lobel (Ed.), *Naming the violence: Speaking out about lesbian battering* (pp. 77-79). Seattle: Seal Press.

Goldner, V. (1992, March/April). Making room for both/and. *Family Therapy Networker*, pp. 54-61.

Goldner, V., Penn, P., Sheinberg, M., & Walker, G. (1990). Love and violence: Gender paradoxes in volatile attachments. *Family Process, 29*, 343-363.

Gonsiorek, J.C. (1985). *A guide to therapy with gay and lesbian clients*. New York: Harrington Park Press.

Haley, J., & Madanes, C. (1992, November). *Working with violent and abusive families*. Paper presented at the Family Therapy Workshops, Rochester, New York.

Hammond, N. (1989). Lesbian victims of relationship violence. In E.D. Rothblum & E. Cole (Eds.), *Loving boldly: Issues facing lesbians* (pp. 89-105). New York: Harrington Park Press.

Hammond, N. (1986). Lesbian victims and the reluctance to identify abuse. In K. Lobel (Ed.), *Naming the violence: Speaking out about lesbian battering* (pp. 190-197). Seattle: Seal Press.

Hart, B. (1986). Lesbian battering: An examination. In K. Lobel (Ed.), *Naming the violence: Speaking out about lesbian battering* (pp. 173-189). Seattle: Seal Press.

Island, D., & Letellier, P. (1991). *Men who beat the men who love them: Battered gay men and domestic violence*. New York: Harrington Park Press.

MacKinnon, L.K., & Miller, D. (1987). The new epistemology and the Milan approach: Feminist and sociopolitical considerations. *Journal of Marital and Family Therapy, 13*, 139-155.

Madanes, C. (1990). *Sex, love, and violence: Strategies for transformation*. New York: W.W. Norton.

Margolin, G. (1982). Ethical and legal considerations in marital and family therapy. *American Psychologist, 37*, 788-801.

Margolin, G., Fernandez, V., Talovic, S., & Onorato, R. (1983). Sex role consider-ations and behavioral marital therapy: Equal does not mean identical. *Journal of Marital and Family Therapy, 9,* 131-145.

Porat, N. (1986). Support groups for battered lesbians. In K. Lobel (Ed.), *Naming the violence: Speaking out about lesbian battering* (pp. 80-87). Seattle: Seal Press.

Pressman, B. (1989). Wife-abused couples: The need for comprehensive theoreti-cal perspectives and integrated treatment models. *Journal of Feminist Family Therapy, 1,* 23-44.

Renzetti, C.M. (1992). *Violent betrayal: Partner abuse in lesbian relationships.* Newbury Park, CA: Sage Publications.

Schechter, S. (1987). *Guidelines for mental health practitioners in domestic vio-lence cases.* Washington, DC: National Coalition Against Domestic Violence.

Silverstein, C. (Ed.). (1991). *Gays, lesbians, and their therapists: Studies in psychotherapy.* New York: W.W. Norton.

Taylor, J.W. (1984). Structured conjoint therapy for spouse abuse cases. *Journal of Contemporary Social Work, 65,* 11-18.

Willback, D. (1989). Ethics and family therapy: The case management of family violence. *Journal of Marital and Family Therapy, 5,* 43-52.

Clinical Models for the Treatment of Gay Male Perpetrators of Domestic Violence

Dan Byrne

SUMMARY. Violence and abuse within same sex relationships have not received the attention they merit as significant psychosocial health issues. The lesbian and gay community has reached a developmental milestone which allows critical examination of same sex relationships and the identification of problems which include physical, emotional, and psychological violence. A literature review reveals a dearth of articles on violence within same sex relationships. External and internalized homophobia are cited as factors which may contribute to low self-esteem experienced by gay males who may be abusive in their relationships. Intervention models described are individual psychosocial treatment, individual psychotherapeutic treatment, and group treatment. *[Article copies available from The Haworth Document Delivery Service: 1-800-342-9678.]*

Dan Byrne, MSW, LICSW, is a board-certified diplomate-clinical social worker, who is employed by the Commission on Mental Health Services and is in private practice in Washington, DC. He founded Rehoboth Institute, which specializes in clinical services for lesbian and gay survivors and perpetrators of violence and abuse.

Correspondence may be addressed to the author at P.O. Box 15372, Washington, DC 20003-0372.

[Haworth co-indexing entry note]: "Clinical Models for the Treatment of Gay Male Perpetrators of Domestic Violence." Byrne, Dan. Co-published simultaneously in *Journal of Gay & Lesbian Social Services* (The Haworth Press, Inc.) Vol. 4, No. 1, 1996, pp. 107-116; and: *Violence in Gay and Lesbian Domestic Partnerships* (ed: Claire M. Renzetti, and Charles Harvey Miley), The Haworth Press, Inc., 1996, pp. 107-116; and: *Violence in Gay and Lesbian Domestic Partnerships* (ed: Claire M. Renzetti, and Charles Harvey Miley) Harrington Park Press, an imprint of The Haworth Press, Inc., 1996, pp. 107-116. Single or multiple copies of this article are available from The Haworth Document Delivery Service [1-800-342-9678, 9:00 a.m. - 5:00 p.m. (EST)].

INTRODUCTION

Over the past ten years, the lesbian and gay community, their organizations, service clubs, clinics, and health services have made great strides to offer comprehensive services to those persons experiencing HIV infection and chemical substance addictions. However, domestic violence within the lesbian and gay community has received scant attention and service provision during the same period of time. Yet, violence within intimate lesbian and gay relationships affects thousands of people and can have lethal consequences. The large number of lesbian and gay persons affected by this psychosocial health problem begs the attention of the community. Recognition by the lesbian/gay community that violence between intimates is a serious problem that is resolvable is the first step towards developing the kinds of services needed by victims and perpetrators. Minimization and denial of the existence of violence within lesbian and gay relationships as well as the magnitude of the problem can be seen as a developmental issue or challenge to the lesbian/gay community.

During the past 25 years, resources and strategies have been directed toward combatting the discrimination and oppression visited on our community by heterosexist American laws (and their selective enforcement or non-enforcement), culture, and values. Since 1980, the HIV and substance abuse epidemics also have demanded massive mobilization, attention, money, and commitment to address these health issues that have ravaged our communities. Identifying and addressing the multitude of issues associated with hate crimes perpetrated against gay and lesbian individuals and institutions have also demanded and received resources. As the acceptance and legitimacy of intimate relationships grow among lesbians and gays as well as heterosexual society, heightened attention and interest are focused on the strengths, diversity, and problems experienced by lesbian and gay couples.

Historically and developmentally, the lesbian and gay community is now able to begin to accept the fact that physical, emotional, and psychological violence is a factor in many of our intimate relationships. Moreover, we have a responsibility to victims and perpetrators of violence within intimate relationships, as well as to our community, to design, implement, and evaluate effective and comprehensive intervention and preventive services. It is the author's firm conviction that the lesbian/gay community can and will assume a national leadership position in promoting intervention and prevention strategies and services, as it has led the nation in shaping and providing services to persons affected by the HIV epidemic. This conviction is based on our capacity to share, discuss, argue, acknowledge differences, and, finally, determine what we want to do and how we want to do it; not relying on an indifferent and homophobic macro society to tell us how to live and how to solve our problems.

LITERATURE REVIEW

A review of the literature reveals that few articles have been written on the subject of violent behavior in same-sex relationships. Even less has been written on the dynamics of the behavior and effective treatment methods for the elimination and/or reduction of violent behaviors, or the prevention of abusive behavior before it presents in a relationship.

Farley (1992) suggests that lesbian and gay perpetrators referred for treatment were often abused themselves or lived in families where members perpetrated physical, emotional, and psychological abuse. Klinger (1991) presented a case study of a lesbian patient, emotionally abused as a child by her mother, who was in treatment because of physically abusing her partner.

MODELS OF TREATMENT

External and Internalized Homophobia

A common characteristic often identified in lesbian and gay perpetrators of abuse in intimate relationships is internalized feelings of self-hate and fear due to one's homosexuality. This can be called internalized homophobia. It is the author's contention that this fear and self-loathing, experienced consciously and unconsciously, emanates from a heterosexist culture and value system which psychically assault and denigrate lesbians and gays from the day of their birth (external homophobia). Homophobia, perpetrated by an often hostile dominant heterosexual society and internalized by gays and lesbians, may be a relevant factor when notions of self-concept and self-esteem are considered (Maiuro et al., 1988; Saunders, 1982; Walker, 1979).

Over the past several years, the majority of gay males referred to the author because of behaving abusively in intimate relationships have manifested a negative self-concept related to being homosexual, as well as negative feelings about who they are as a person. In the initial stages of treatment, it is not uncommon that abusive gay males (and abusive heterosexual males) experience marked difficulty identifying positive personal characteristics or attributes. Most, however, have no difficulty identifying negative personal characteristics. They tend to perceive themselves as bad persons rather than persons with intrinsic worth who have learned or exhibited inappropriate behaviors. An example of this is the following. Early in treatment, the author frequently asks patients to spontaneously name three positive characteristics or personal strengths. Most patients either cannot identify three positive attributes or cannot do so quickly. On the other hand, when asked to cite three negative characteristics, the same patients do so rapidly and often exceed the requested number.

A critical question or theme woven into all models of treatment discussed below and posed to clients is: How is it that you are hurting so badly and experiencing such pain that you are abusing your partner? Another theme common to all treatment models and reiterated frequently is that positive change is possible: Emotional, cognitive, and behavioral transformations can be made, accomplished by a commitment to end abusive behavior in intimate relationships, honesty, accountability, commitment to unlearn destructive cognitive patterns and behaviors and learn assertive, constructive, and responsible methods of dealing with tension, conflict, and feelings in intimate relationships.

Individual Psychosocial Treatment

This treatment model focuses on behavioral changes and the acquisition of new skills. It is time-limited, usually 12 to 30 sessions. The author has found that scheduling 2 sessions weekly for the first few weeks facilitates the intervention process and tends to underscore the seriousness of the abusive behavior. While 2-stage group treatment (didactic and long-term group psychotherapy) with concomitant individual therapy is the author's clinical treatment of choice, individual psychosocial treatment is often used in locations which do not have comprehensive services for gay males who are abusive in intimate relationships.

The goal of treatment is to create, nurture, and strengthen the individual's capacity to maintain intimate relationships which are free of violent and abusive behavior. Treatment begins with a signed, written contract from the client to not perpetrate emotional, psychological, and physical violence within the current or any subsequent relationships and to immediately report any abusive incidents to the therapist. Written contracts can be a useful tool for the client to accept complete accountability and responsibility for abusive behavior regardless of provocation.

An individualized safety plan, which is shared with the partner for his information and comment, also needs to be formulated in the beginning sessions. The safety plan should include details on time-out procedures which ensure the safety of the partner, the client, and others. Three rules which should be included in any safety plan are to not drink, use drugs, or drive a vehicle. Safety plan procedures should also include specific details on the duration of the time-out, communication with the partner prior to returning home, and any customized elements which are particular to the client's situation. When the client is feeling violent towards his partner or feels a loss of self-control, he needs to follow his safety plan.

Initial sessions should also focus on collecting information that leads to a comprehensive psychosocial assessment. Particular attention should be paid to obtaining a history of violent or abusive behaviors perpetrated by the client as an adult. For example, does the client force or coerce his partner to have sexual relations against his will, demand participation in sexual behavior that the partner does not like, or is the client sexually assaultive with his partner? Family history should be obtained with attention paid to abuse or violent behavior witnessed by the client in his family of origin or experienced by him. This includes severe physical punishment, sexual abuse, or emotional neglect. Sexual identity and orientation issues ought to be explored as well as the client's psychological comfort or discomfort with being gay, i.e., is being gay perceived as a positive aspect of identity or experienced as dystonic to the client's identity?

The psychosocial assessment can provide clues to the therapist regarding the degree and intensity of internalized homophobia experienced by the client. The client can be referred to a support group that focuses on coming out and positive gay identity issues, another therapist if he wants to explore issues that surface during the psychosocial assessment, or re-contract with his present clinician.

Middle sessions focus on the identification and recognition of thoughts, feelings, and physiological cues which occur prior to the manifestation of violent behavior. The author has found that abusive gay males (and abusive heterosexual males) often need assistance in identifying, experiencing, and owning feelings and can greatly benefit from a hand-out list of feelings. As the client develops enhanced recognition of maladaptive and destructive patterns which have resulted in abusive behavior, he may become more amenable to considering different ways of thinking, feeling, and behaving. Non-violent, assertive, and respectful alternatives can be elicited from the client. New ways to think, feel, and act can also be introduced by the therapist, discussed in sessions with the client, and practiced with the clinician, for example, in role play.

Closing sessions review, reinforce, and refine positive behavioral changes and competencies accomplished by the client during treatment. Assertive communication, active listening, and the identification, awareness and expression of feelings are skills that require constant practice and honing in order to be internalized and used productively and routinely. The author has clients engage in "bragging" exercises with regard to naming positive attributes they identify within themselves and also encourages clients to practice positive self-talk, especially when confronted by a situation or event that has elicited an abusive or inappropriate response in the past.

Closing sessions are also forums to discuss community resources that can support the client in his efforts to maintain and strengthen positive cognitive and behavioral gains. Persons and resources that can be called upon during times of crisis should be identified and preliminary contact should occur. The author recommends identifying a "special buddy" or friend, trusted by the client and his partner, who can be contacted before or during a stressful period, thus breaking the isolation often experienced by the abusive partner and the person victimized by the abuse. Finally, the author has found that organized recreational/sports activities are a safe way to discharge tension and energy.

Individual Psychotherapeutic Treatment

Psychotherapeutic treatment for a gay male who is abusive in an intimate relationship is divided into two stages, a 12- to 20- week educational phase (with a crisis intervention component if indicated) and a psychotherapeutic stage that can range from 6 months to 2 1/2 years.

As in the psychosocial model, treatment begins with the completion of a questionnaire that elicits information on the client's abusive and violent behavior towards his partner, discussion about the behavior, and a verbal commitment from the client not to behave abusively and violently. A written contract that proscribes violent and abusive behavior in the relationship is then presented to the client for discussion and signature. The contract also stipulates that any abusive or violent behavior that does occur must be reported promptly to the therapist.

Homicidal and suicidal ideation should be assessed early in the initial stage of treatment. An instrument to assess self-esteem also can be administered early in treatment. Subsequent self-esteem assessment can also occur in later points in the therapeutic process if indicated. The author's clinical experience suggests that many patients may identify treatment goals that, in the short run, are unrealistic and, therefore, may be a prelude for "failure" and premature termination of therapy. The therapeutic process is well served by the clinician keeping the treatment focus on supporting the patient's efforts to cease physically violent behavior by using time-outs and a customized safety plan.

The second stage of this psychotherapeutic model focuses on intrapsychic phenomena and the exploration of feelings. It is important that the clinician elicits a comprehensive developmental history from the client that illuminates any patterns of abuse or neglect observed or experienced by the patient, i.e., if the client witnessed physically or emotionally abusive behavior in parental interactions or experienced severe corporal punishment. These events and their sequelae, as well as the associated feelings, need to be explored and worked through in a sensitive manner.

Not infrequently, the therapist finds that he or she is working with an abusive client who has a history of being abused himself. The developmental history should elicit information on any abandonment issues, the emotional availability of the client's parents, discipline practices, power and control dynamics within the family of origin, communication styles, shame practices, sibling relationships, dating practices, peer relationships, adolescent and adult relationships, role expectations, intimacy issues, sexual feelings and expression, abusive behavior patterns, and identity and sexual orientation issues. The author's clinical experience suggests that the majority of gay male patients seeking therapy because of behaving abusively in intimate relationships feel negatively about their homosexual orientation.

Experiences and issues associated with external and internal homophobia should be addressed. A therapeutic objective is the gradual transformation of a negative self-concept fueled by self-hate and internalized homophobia to a positive self-concept that affirms a healthy gay identity and creates an internal structure that supports the development of self-esteem.

Information obtained from the developmental history can also yield strengths, competencies, and areas of skill of which the client is not consciously aware, that can be marshalled to support efforts to modify perceptions and abusive behaviors as well as support efforts to perceive and respond to stressors and provocation in an assertive, controlled, and non-injurious manner. The client's negotiation and compromise skills may need to be explored and strengthened, thus offering alternatives to power struggles and confrontation. Finally, the second stage of treatment focuses on the client's capacity to identify, own, and accept his perceptions, feelings, and actions.

Group Treatment

The selection of group treatment as the preferred intervention for heterosexual males who behave abusively in intimate relationships is well-documented in the literature (Edleson & Grusznski, 1989; Edleson, Miller, Stone, & Chapman, 1985; Gondolf, 1985; Stordeur & Stille, 1989). The preference by clinicians of group treatment for gay males, abusive in intimate relationships, is not well-documented in the literature, but Farley in Seattle and Shattuck in San Francisco, as well as other clinicians who treat abusive gay males, feel group treatment is preferred; group treatment with individual treatment is ideal. This seems to be particularly true when the client has been able to establish trust and feel acceptance from group leaders and members.

Individual treatment can occur prior, during, or after group treatment. In some situations, a group may not be available at the time a client is ready to begin treatment, group treatment may be initially refused by the client, or he initially may not be able to tolerate or be too disruptive in group therapy. Concurrent treatment may be indicated when the patient's own historical experiences with physical, sexual, or emotional abuse, previously repressed or denied, begin to surface. In addition, issues around internalized homophobia and its sequelae may present and may need individual attention. Individual treatment may also occur after group treatment has ended. The patient may desire to explore personal issues that surfaced during the term of the group. The patient, after participating in group treatment, may also feel more curious or empowered about himself and seek additional therapy.

REFERENCES

Edleson, J.L., Miller, D.M., Stone, G.W., & Chapman, D.G. (1985). Group treatment for men who batter. *Social Work Research and Abstracts, 21,* 18-21.

Edleson, J.L., & Grusznski, R.J. (1989). Treating men who batter: Four years of outcome data from the Domestic Abuse Project. *Journal of Social Service Research, 12,* 3-22.

Farley, N. (1992). Same sex domestic violence. In S.H. Dworkin & F.J. Gutierrez (Eds.), *Counseling gay men and lesbians: Journey to the end of the rainbow* (pp. 231-242). Alexandria, VA: AACD Press.

Gondolf, E.W. (1985). *Men who batter: An integrated approach for stopping wife abuse.* Holmes Beach, FL: Learning Publications, Inc.

Klinger, R.L. (1991). Treatment of a lesbian batterer. In C. Silverstein (Ed.), *Gays, lesbians, and their therapists* (pp. 126-142). New York: W.W. Norton.

Maiuro, R.D., Cahn, T.S., Vitaliano, P.P., Wagner, B.C., & Zegree, J.B. (1988).

Anger, hostility, and depression in domestically violent versus generally assaultive men and non-violent control subjects. *Journal of Consulting and Clinical Psychology, 56,* 17-23.

Saunders, D.G. (1982). Counseling the violent husband. In P.A. Keller & G. Ritt (Eds.), *Innovations in clinical practice: A sourcebook, Vol. 1* (pp. 16-29). Sarasota, FL: Professional Resource Exchange.

Stordeur, R.A., & Stille, R. (1989). *Ending men's violence against their partners: One road to peace.* Newbury Park, CA: Sage Publications, Inc.

Walker, L.E. (1979). *The battered woman.* New York: Harper & Row.

Index

Haworth
DOCUMENT DELIVERY
SERVICE

This valuable service provides a single-article order form for any article from a Haworth journal.

- *Time Saving:* No running around from library to library to find a specific article.
- *Cost Effective:* All costs are kept down to a minimum.
- *Fast Delivery:* Choose from several options, including same-day FAX.
- *No Copyright Hassles:* You will be supplied by the original publisher.
- *Easy Payment:* Choose from several easy payment methods.

Open Accounts Welcome for . . .
- Library Interlibrary Loan Departments
- Library Network/Consortia Wishing to Provide Single-Article Services
- Indexing/Abstracting Services with Single Article Provision Services
- Document Provision Brokers and Freelance Information Service Providers

---

MAIL or *FAX* THIS ENTIRE ORDER FORM TO:

Haworth Document Delivery Service
The Haworth Press, Inc.
10 Alice Street
Binghamton, NY 13904-1580

or FAX: 1-800-895-0582
or CALL: 1-800-342-9678
9am-5pm EST

PLEASE SEND ME PHOTOCOPIES OF THE FOLLOWING SINGLE ARTICLES:
1) Journal Title: _____
   Vol/Issue/Year:_____Starting & Ending Pages:_____
Article Title:_____
_____

2) Journal Title: _____
   Vol/Issue/Year:_____Starting & Ending Pages:_____
Article Title:_____
_____

3) Journal Title: _____
   Vol/Issue/Year:_____Starting & Ending Pages:_____
Article Title:_____
_____

4) Journal Title: _____
   Vol/Issue/Year:_____Starting & Ending Pages:_____
Article Title:_____
_____

(See other side for Costs and Payment Information)

COSTS: Please figure your cost to order quality copies of an article.

1. Set-up charge per article: $8.00
   ($8.00 × number of separate articles) _____

2. Photocopying charge for each article:

   1-10 pages: $1.00 _____

   11-19 pages: $3.00 _____

   20-29 pages: $5.00 _____

   30+ pages: $2.00/10 pages _____

3. Flexicover (optional): $2.00/article _____

4. Postage & Handling: US: $1.00 for the first article/
   $.50 each additional article _____

   Federal Express: $25.00 _____

   Outside US: $2.00 for first article/
   $.50 each additional article _____

5. Same-day FAX service: $.35 per page _____

   GRAND TOTAL: _____

METHOD OF PAYMENT: (please check one)

❑ Check enclosed   ❑ Please ship and bill. PO # _____
(sorry we can ship and bill to bookstores only! All others must pre-pay)

❑ Charge to my credit card: ❑ Visa; ❑ MasterCard; ❑ Discover;
   ❑ American Express;

Account Number: _____ Expiration date: _____

Signature: ✗ _____

Name: _____ Institution: _____

Address: _____

_____

City: _____ State: _____ Zip: _____

Phone Number: _____ FAX Number: _____

MAIL or *FAX* THIS ENTIRE ORDER FORM TO:

Haworth Document Delivery Service | **or FAX:** 1-800-895-0582
The Haworth Press, Inc. | **or CALL:** 1-800-342-9678
10 Alice Street | 9am-5pm EST)
Binghamton, NY 13904-1580 |